Embracing Your Best Self

Nancy Zimmerman

DEDICATION

I dedicate this book to God – who has shown me the face of I AM THAT I AM and has inspired my journey and continues with me.

To my son, Andrew, and my daughter, Allison
To my grandchildren:

       Elijah, Cheyenne, and Gideon

You have all shown me the faces of Love, Joy, Excitement, and Patience.

ACKNOWLEDGMENTS

I would like to thank Carolyn Dupas, Glenda Butler, and Sandra Slaven for including me in their sisterhood. I am fortunate indeed to count these ageless women among my friends.

A very BIG thank you goes to Donna Reagan, whose editorial expertise helped me greatly with this book. She offered evaluation, suggestions, and encouragement, and I appreciate it more than I can say.

Another BIG "Thank you" goes to Audrey Carie for the wonderful cover art. She is a rare and talented young woman and I am so glad that I have been a part of her life as it has unfolded.

Another round of thanks goes to my son, Andrew Zimmerman Jones for all of his technical assistance in getting this from my computer to the "cyber powers-that-be" in order to make this publication possible.

It would be impossible for me to list everyone and everything for which I am so grateful. I am thankful for everyone who contributed to my thoughts and ideas, either directly or indirectly. I will say that all of my Facebook friends have provided me with Inspirational sites and wisdom that has come at the exact moment that I have needed it. Some of you I have known personally for years, some I have known personally for a short period of time, and some you I have never met and may never meet personally. You are all an important thread in the tapestry of my life. Thank you so very much.

There are countless others that I wish to acknowledge for their inspiration, realizing that the list could never include everyone.

I would like to thank authors who contributed words of wisdom, understanding, and inspiration along my journey to "me." These include Dr. Wayne Dyer, Neale Donald Walsch, Philip Gulley, Debbie Macomber, Deepak Chopra, His Holiness the XIV Dalai Lama, Robert Twyman, Neville Goddard, Uell S. Anderson, Timber Hawkeye, and Eckhart Tolle, to name a few.

I have drawn from the inspirational quotes of the Dalai Lama, Albert Einstein, John Lennon, George Carlin, Bill Cosby, Oprah Winfrey, Dr. Martin Luther King, Jr., Ralph Waldo Emerson, Fred Rogers, Mother

Teresa, Carl Sagan, Neil DeGrasse Tyson, Will Smith, and Henry David Thoreau, among others.

I cannot even begin to acknowledge the scope of the music that sends my soul flying. Much inspiration has come to me from the Sirius Satellite Radio and the Classical Pops channel as I have driven along, lost in thought. As I actually sat and wrote, Liberace, Michael Buble, Frank Sinatra, Dean Martin, Roger Williams, The Mills Brothers, Sheena Easton, Patsy Cline, Willie Nelson, Luciano Pavarotti, and Little Richard have kept me company.

The art work and photographs of nature that have crossed my Facebook pages and have accompanied the inspirational messages have been phenomenal. There are some talented and gifted people out there who have generously shared that talent whose names I shall probably never know, but I thank them more than I can express. The sculpting creations of Angelika Seik have crossed my pages and served to inspire me because of the great talent required to see the possibilities of beauty in a piece of stone.

I want to thank everyone who has been in my life for this journey. Without each and every experience and interaction, I would not be who I am today, and would not be where I am today. Although I originally thought this journey began in a casino, it began the day I was born, at least this physical incarnation. It was the experience at the casino that opened the door into a different realm for me. I hope you enjoy this book and that it gives you a catalyst for looking at your life, for looking at how you are spending all of your "now's", and for having the courage to step away from any of your fears into a more fulfilling life, regardless of where you are on your journey.

INTRODUCTION

I have experienced an amazing two years. I took a trip, met a new friend; then, I began re-examining my life and how I wanted to spend the rest of it. I read and read, found author after author and inspiration after inspiration that caused me to ask question after question. This book begins the story of my awakening, my enlightenment, my understanding of what I am doing on the planet. It is a journey that has taken me from a negative, disillusioned individual who was leading a lonely, uncomfortable, and unrewarding life to someone who looks forward to every day, knowing that each one will be better than the one before.

It is a story that is, in some ways, radical. It caused me to go places that made me uncomfortable. It caused me to examine my past, to accept my past, and to be thankful for all the past experiences that have brought me to this point. I was able to look at certain circumstances and my reaction to them without self-loathing and regret. I now see that my reactions were what they needed to be for me to get to where I am now.

This book isn't trying to convince anyone of anything. It is simply an account of the wanderings of my mind. What has happened to me came about as a result of some experiences and how I reacted to them. It is about how I went from disappointment and unhappiness in life to a contented, joyous individual, ready to live life and embrace all that life is about, the highs and lows, and come out with a feeling of peace. I have drawn information from many sources and I am attempting to put them all together for you as I assimilated them for me. It is my sincerest desire that you are all able to take what I am saying and use it in some way to make your life the very best that it can become.

Nothing that I have included is new. Others have traversed similar paths from different origins to different destinations. Every path is valuable and every path is unique. I have not discovered some "magic bullet" that will insure that your life will miraculously be filled with only wonderful experiences. Every experience has the potential to be perceived as "good" or "bad" depending on your choice of how you are going to view it. What I am offering is a glimpse into my life, a chance to see real examples of how shifts can occur; and, once they begin, become a way of life that you only want to keep enjoying.

I hope you enjoy this book. It is my desire that, as you read, you find yourself deciding to get a pen and underline a few things. That you decide this is a book you might want to give as a gift or recommend to a friend. I hope you chuckle in places. I will understand if there is an occasional tear, there were many as I wrote it. If you have questions or comments and would like to correspond, my e-mail address is: nzimmie@gmail.com I will be excited to hear from you, and bring you into my life experience. I know we will both benefit from the association.

The inspiration for this book came from an act of kindness and generosity. That is how this particular leg of my journey will end. Fifty percent of the net profits from the sale of this book will go to Heifer International. If you are not familiar with their organization, they provide animals to families in different communities around the world to help provide a food source and a source of income. Heifer instructs the people receiving this gift on how to take care of the animal and utilize what it has to offer. The family then passes along the first born of that gift on to another family, instructing them on the care of the animal… And the gift keeps on giving. Families and communities around the world benefit from these gifts which address needs physically, financially and culturally. If you want to learn more, you can at: www.heiferinternational.com

CHAPTER ONE

There are times in our life that we reflect upon with speculation. Many women question what their children would be like if they had chosen a different partner. Right now, I am wondering how differently my life might have turned out if I had not wanted the dorm room overlooking the campus quad.

It was a muggy July 4th in the summer of 2011. I was sitting on my "deckio"- a cross between a concrete patio and a wooden deck, in that it was concrete but was raised with a wrought iron railing around it. My cousin and I had dubbed that name when I first moved to Anderson because I have a patio and a deck both in the front of the house and this was just an easier way to refer to this space. I was sitting on the deckio sipping peach tea when I began thinking of Carolyn. She and I had been college roommates in the late sixties. I hadn't liked her at all but she had the best room in the dorm, the one that overlooked the campus quad. You could see who was out with whom and what they were doing. My first roommate had been a disaster and my second hadn't been much better. Carolyn was due to graduate mid-year of the next year so I figured I could put up with her for one term. I wanted that room!! After we became really good friends, I told her about my pre-judgment of her and we have laughed about it often. I really had no reason not to like her, but didn't figure I needed one. She had a soft Tennessee accent, was pretty, and everyone like her. I needed no other reasons in my mind.

After college, she was visiting her sister, Glenda, in New Orleans and met Al. They were married and I visited them a few times while she lived there. I had met Glenda but their other sister, Sandy, lived there also and we had never met. When Hurricane Katrina blew through, all three of the sisters moved back to Tennessee. Glenda and Sandy were there briefly and went back to New Orleans but Carolyn, who had been widowed for several years, stayed in Tennessee. Glenda later retired and moved back also, but Sandy stayed.

It had been probably two years since I had talked to Carolyn and decided to phone her that day. She is the kind of friend one seldom gets in life, the kind you can go years without talking to, then when you do talk, it is like you visited just last week. We chatted, laughed, and caught up on our lives since we had last spoken.

As we were winding down our conversation, we went to the usual, "We really do have to get together," chatter that friends do. It is a sincere desire, but we often don't go ahead and make plans. That day we decided that we just needed to set a date to visit. She said that it had been a while since she had gone to New Orleans to visit Sandy so that is where we decided to go in October.

Carolyn lives near Nashville, TN, about a seven hour drive from me. It was decided that I would drive down there, spend the night, and we would take off the next morning for the nine hour drive that would get us to our destination. It was as though we were in our twenties again as we visited all the way to New Orleans. Sandy had reserved a room for us at Harrah's casino for the three nights that we would be there. We arrived, met Sandy, checked in and went across the street to play the slots.

Casinos had never held much appeal to me. I had never understood the machines. I would put my money in a machine (I figured they were all the same) and the next thing I knew the money was gone. It wasn't fun, in my opinion, but I knew lots of people who liked it, so there must be some aspect of it that I had not discovered. Carolyn and Sandy explained the machines to me. I watched them play then I sat and played, still not quite understanding, either when I won or when I lost, exactly what was happening. My money didn't last long.

Sandy reached into her purse and pulled out a one-hundred dollar bill. She reached over and stuck it in the machine that I was sitting at right next to her. "Here," she said, "play this." I told her that I couldn't do that. It was about the amount that I had brought to last me for three days and I had already lost it in one evening. She then said, "Just play it and have fun with it! Fun! Fun! Fun!"

Well, I did play, and I did have fun, but I did lose it. She did the same thing again. I couldn't believe it. Once again, she said to just have fun. That money lasted me for quite a while, but eventually lost that too. Luckily, ATMs are available and I was able to get money out to pay her back and to continue to learn more about the machines on a much more conservative path. The first "Casino lesson" that I learned was: If you keep playing long enough, eventually you will go to zero!

The thing that struck me at that point in time, that I did not know was going to affect me so deeply, was how generous that woman was. She didn't know me. She didn't "loan" me the money, she gave it to me. In all the years I had known Carolyn, I had never met Sandy. Here she was, sharing generously, not knowing whether I would ever pay her back. Then something even more amazing occurred to me… she didn't care. She was giving because that is what she does, that is who she is.

Another thing I realized during that trip and the time I spent with Carolyn and Sandy was that some people just have fun in life. They enjoy themselves regardless of the circumstances. I had experienced a lot of enjoyable times in my life, but they were usually tinged with anticipating the next enjoyable time and not taking full advantage of the time right then. Fun was something I had on occasion but not a daily life experience. I kind of had to force it. The three days we spent were full of fun, laughter, and enjoyment.

The second afternoon we were there, Sandy met us after work in a different area of the casino. While we were walking through the machines, she motioned to me and said, "Come over here and take a look at this." What I saw was a five hundred dollar machine. I just couldn't imagine, and still can't, someone putting five hundred dollars in a slot machine for a one time shot to win. I made the comment that if someone had five hundred dollars to put in a machine like that, I hoped they gave five thousand away to help people. I felt like anyone with that kind of money should be willing to go above and beyond to help others. I still do.

Those episodes at the casino stayed with me after I came home. I had already started making some changes in my life and those changes, combined with the New Orleans experience served as a jumping off place for some incredibly transforming experiences. There is a saying that when the student is ready, the teachers will appear. I believe these things had an impact on me because I was at a point in my life where I was ready to be impacted. I believe that people and events are put in our lives as we are ready for them and since that experience, I have come to find that to be true more and more often. There are no coincidences in life.

CHAPTER TWO

I grew up in southern Indiana in the nineteen-fifties. I was the older of two, with my sister being three and a half years younger. I remember getting a television set and watching the "Cisco Kid", "Sky King," and "Rin Tin Tin." I also remember watching wrestling and roller derby. The educational show we had was "Miss Frances and her Ding Dong School." I was a fan of "Howdy Doody" and "The Mickey Mouse Club." The television was black and white. I was in the eighth grade when I went to a friend's house and watched "Bonanza" in color! I will never forget the magnificence of seeing that orange flame burning that map as Adam, Hoss, Little Joe and Ben rode into the picture. There are some things that happen to us in life that we just never forget, and that was one of my times.

When I was about four years old, my mother, a teacher, said that it was just easier to teach me to read than it was to continually be telling me words. I have always been an avid reader. I also had a love of numbers and knew my math facts and the basics of addition and subtraction when I went to school. There was not a kindergarten at the country school I attended. I was six years old. After three weeks, it was decided that I would be moved to the second grade because I already knew what others would learn in the first grade. I was a chunky six year old. I had always been at home with my mother and sister so I was not socialized the way the others were who had already been in school for a year. I was immature and it was a recipe for disaster. The other kids were resentful that this "baby" was put in their class. Although I didn't struggle academically, it was difficult for me to find acceptance.

As I grew up, I continued to struggle with acceptance by my peers. I seemed to have no control over my external environment, so I turned to food as a source of comfort, and as a source of something I could control. Because I enjoyed reading so much, I was sedentary. Other kids were out running around, playing with each other. I was sitting, by myself, reading. My world was wherever I wanted it to be when I read. If I were compared to students of today, I would appear to be quite average, but in the fifties, there were a lot of "skinny" kids, and I was not one of them. This bit of insecurity was fueled by comments I often heard at home, "You would be so pretty if only you would lose weight." The more I heard the comment, the more the feelings of insecurity, inferiority, and lack of acceptance made their way into my mind, and more I ate.

When I was a freshman in high school, plans were made for school districts to begin consolidation the following year. My parents decided that since my mother taught in Princeton, it would be a good time for my sister and me to go ahead and enroll there. The first consolidation would last two years and then the entire section of the county would go into Princeton. It was wonderful. I walked through the doors and was accepted by the other students as a new kid they would like to meet. There were no old reminders that I was the youngest person in the class. I was free to be me and for the first time, I enjoyed making friends easily. I began to recognize that I was friendly, well-liked, and out-going. The kids I ran around with were not gossipy and took no time or delight in belittling others. It was an exceptional time for me, but I was still concerned about my size and appearance. I was average when I look back at the pictures of me during high school, but I was always worrying about what I ate, what I weighed, and what size clothes I wore.

I had this on-going love/hate relationship with food. My view of my body was so skewed that I based my value on what my body looked like. I saw it as my enemy – not worthy of my respect, only my hatred. When I could lose a few pounds, I felt good, I felt happy. When I gained a few pounds, I felt miserable and worthless. I had no idea what I even looked like to others, my own view was so messed up. I went on diets and got pills from the doctor to help curb my appetite. We know now they were amphetamines and they are illegal--not so in the sixties when I was a teen.

CHAPTER THREE

In the summer of 2009, my son, Andrew, gave me the audio tape *Excuses Begone!* by Dr. Wayne Dyer. I listened to it on my way to Florida and was introduced to the term "memes" (rhymes with genes). Memes are the thoughts and beliefs you hold that spread like a virus in your mind. We believe these memes to be true and they can limit our abilities in life. Because we believe them to be true, we don't question their validity, nor do we believe that we have any control over them.

I began to realize that the messages I had received about my size from my mother might just be based on the messages she felt that she had received. She had always expressed that she grew up heavy and not very pretty. The pictures I saw of her were lovely. She was about 5'7" tall and her sister was barely 5 feet tall. Her best friend was also about that height. They both weighed about 90 pounds. Next to them, my mother would have felt like an Amazon. Her view of her body influenced how she related to my body size. The viruses in her mind were passed to me.

This gave my daughter, Allison, and me much to discuss on the trip to Florida, while we were in Florida, and on the way back home. We listened to the discs, one at a time, and discussed them before going to the next disc. The terms memes became personal and I talked about the memes I carried with me and we discussed her memes, some of which I had contributed. It made for some very interesting conversations.

When we went to Florida that year, it was a special time. In 1985 I had purchased a time share on Sanibel Island. I had visions of yearly family trips there with kids, spouses, and grandchildren. This was the first time that our newly expanded family had spent more than four or five hours together. What was I thinking? Seven days and nights?? There had been some significant problems issues with Allison when Cheyenne (my grand- daughter) was born and Andrew harbored some resentment that I had extended the invitation to her. It was an opportunity for me to spend a week with Cheyenne and mend some fences with Allison, and in that respect, I was okay with the fact that she might very well be "using me" for the trip. She and I had been coming to Sanibel every summer for the previous few years and it always served as a time of healing for us both, regardless of any problems during the year.

It was after this trip that I realized that for me to stay in Vincennes, about an hour away from Evansville where Allison lived, was not going to change anything. If I wanted to be a Nana, it would have to be in Anderson with Andrew and his family.

CHAPTER FOUR

After I got out of college, I began teaching in Crawfordsville, Indiana. Several of my sister's friends were in college at Indiana State in Terre Haute and I would often go down on the weekends to visit and party with them. Although there were some single teachers at the school where I taught, they were in relationships so I really had no one to spend any time with on the weekends. It was during some of these visits that I met Don, a friend of my sister, Mary Ann. We hung out together and he seemed to accept me just as I was. By this time I was what would now be called "big and beautiful"… at the time, I just considered it "fat". We had good times and seemed to gravitate to each other during those times. I had dated very little in high school or college, choosing not to get involved in any relationship until school was out of the way, I was teaching, and making my own living.

I was amazed that anyone could like me romantically at the size that I was, but there was Don. I fell in love, or what I thought love felt like. At the end of that school year, he was going to go to Chicago to spend the summer at his sister's house and work up there to help finance his next year's college expenses. Before he left, he told me that we could only be friends and that any relationship but friendship would have to end. This was not what I wanted to hear, so

I quickly informed him that there would be no friendship. He was never to call me again, unless he had something more than friendship in mind.

It was during this time in the summer that I accepted that a relationship with Don was not going to materialize. I felt that if I wanted to get out into the dating world, I would have to lose some weight. I had moved to Vincennes after accepting a job there for the next year. I joined Weight Watchers and lost about sixty pounds over the next six months. I was gaining confidence but I was not meeting anyone I was attracted to. It was shortly after Halloween that a mutual friend of ours called. He said that he had been to ISU that weekend and talked to Don and he thought Don was going to call me. When he did, I reminded him of our last conversation. He said that he wanted to talk to me and would like to see me the next weekend when he came home for a visit. He told me that he loved me and wanted to marry me. My answer was, "When?" We set the date for the following summer and then we began actually dating.

I continued to lose some weight, but I never felt secure in my relationship with Don. One time my dad told me, when we were arguing, that I had better watch out, "we have to put up with you, but Don doesn't." Well, there was yet another reason for someone else not to care about me when I was just being me. I didn't realize it then, but more messages (and more memes) were still being added to my collection to be revisited over and over.

Don and I married and were divorced eight years later. After the divorce, I had a five year old son and a two-and-a-half year old daughter. I decided to have a duplex built. We would live on one side and I would rent the other side out to help pay the mortgage. It was a good arrangement and worked out very well.

In 1989, I was transferred, involuntarily, to a middle school teaching position. A six-year relationship (also to be shared later) was ending. To deal with both of these events, I turned to my drug of choice—food. I was determined that I would not risk being hurt again and fat is a great buffer. After all, I had enough reminders from my youth that I would be "pretty, if only you would lose weight", so I determined (not consciously, you understand) that if I were fat, I would not be pretty, no one else would want me and I had the rejection problem all taken care of. I did not see that it was a self-rejection before someone else could reject me. Dumb, but it worked. It worked so well that for twenty years I lived a miserable life of self-loathing with my built in excuse for everything that happened to me-it was because I was fat. I judged everyone before they judged me because I knew they would see how worthless I was. I condemned people I didn't know. I criticized everything and everybody. I honestly don't know how I managed to keep friends, but I did.

After the trip to Florida in 2009, I realized that because I had become morbidly obese, I was going to need to get myself located where I had some family nearby. I had developed type-2 diabetes. My joints were overworked and I had difficulty walking because of the weight. I realized my health was at risk but it was not until I had moved and my grandson, Gideon, was born that I realized how debilitating it really was.

CHAPTER FIVE

When I decided to move to Anderson, it was not an easy decision. I had lived in southern Indiana all my life. At that time I had spent thirty-three years teaching in Vincennes. I was retired and spent my time at home working on various hobbies and projects. I was very close to being a hermit and was quite satisfied with it. I determined that I could be a hermit anywhere and Anderson would put me closer to family as I grew older and might need help. I wasn't sure I would like the move, so I kept the duplex after deciding that I could rent both sides out. If I didn't like it in Anderson, I could always move back.

I got moved in about two weeks before Gideon was born. Elijah was four years old at that time and I was really enjoying being a Nana. Amber was wanting to go back to school and get her degree so it was decided by all of us that I would keep Gideon while she attended classes two or three days a week. I was concerned because I had to put Gideon on the ottoman when I got up and actually had to push it around to the dining room and put him in his seat and later into the bouncy. I was afraid to carry him because I was not sure-footed and I didn't want to fall and hurt him. If I fell, I also knew that I probably couldn't get up without help.

By February, I became determined to lose weight. One morning, I just woke up and said to myself, "Today is it. I am getting this excess weight off!!" I had lost weight years earlier with Weight Watchers. For about two years during that time, I had been in charge of meetings and had counseled and encouraged others on weight loss and how to successfully manage their food habits. Because of my fairly recent diabetes diagnosis, I had gone to nutritionists. I knew how to lose weight. It was a matter of making some other adjustments to what I would or would not allow into my body, and I devised a plan. I was going to stick with the plan, I was not going to batter myself about how quickly it was coming off, and I was not going to give up for any reason at any time. I had no doubts about my ability to achieve a significant weight loss.

After two or three days, I looked in the mirror and thought I could tell a difference. After a week, Amber asked me if I was losing weight. After two weeks, my clothes were getting big on me and I was actually able to dig into the closet and get into some things that I had moved with me even though I hadn't worn them in years. I was on my way!

It was about this time that Amber asked me if I wanted to go to a garden club-meeting with her. That was an interest we shared and I had received my Master Gardner certification several years prior. Because I was more self-confident, I jumped at the chance. I met several very nice people there who are still friends. They told me about the Master Gardener group and I decided to go to that. Many of the same people were there. I began making friends and the weight continued to come off.

What I didn't realize, that Amber pointed out, is that I had been using Dr. Dyer's suggestions in *Excuses Begone!* as an approach to the weight loss. I was not allowing the memes that had infected me to continue to take their toll. I bought his book and began reading it. He catalogues eighteen excuses we use and seven principles we can use to get rid of those excuses. I was putting some of those into action.

I was continuing to lose weight and had lost over a hundred pounds by the following year. I was active in the garden club and

Master Gardener's group. It was about this time that I was asked if I wanted to help at an informational booth at one of the local plant sales at a church. Since much of the purpose of Master Gardeners is to help others learn more about gardening, I was happy to. The people I met there were very friendly and when they invited me to come to church any time, I just thought I might give it a try. I had not attended church since I had been divorced on any kind of remotely regular basis. I had tried on occasion to find a church that I would like to attend but I had never felt the friendliness that I found at this one.

I began making friends and getting involved there also. Between the two activities, I was beginning to have a life. I had not been so social since before I was married and I enjoyed it.

It was about this time that the trip with Carolyn to New Orleans took place.

CHAPTER SIX

I really enjoyed my trip to New Orleans and I had more fun than I'd had in years. I decided I was going to the casino in Anderson to see how it compared and I enjoyed it also. Everyone was having a good time and there was usually someone sitting next to me at the slot machine that I got into a conversation with. Invariably, they would tell me about their family, grandkids, problems with their own kids, etc., and I realized that was something that I had noticed that people had always done. They would talk and I would listen. For years I had been told often that I was a good listener, but I guess I never believed it because I saw myself with such negative eyes. (It also might have had to do with the fact that I can be quite a "talker" too.) Even when someone gave me a compliment about anything, it was very difficult to accept. I enjoyed these conversations and figured that they needed someone to talk to so it did me no harm to listen. I also thought that, like me, this might be the only opportunity during the day that they had to listen to the sound of their own voice.

As I sat there in the casino I began thinking about many different things. The generosity of Sandy kept cropping up. Now that I was attending church, there were opportunities for me to help others and occasions to be generous with both my time and money.

I found that it did make me feel better about myself when I helped others in whatever way I could. I noticed that I didn't seem to miss any of the money I gave away. I began to want to do more. I thought about that five hundred dollar machine, too. Perhaps, if I had any money to spend at the casino, maybe I had more to give away. I wanted to find a way to apply those thoughts and ideas to my life. I wanted to do something unexpected for someone.

Christmas was getting closer and one day I was in a bookstore looking around. There was a book by Debbie Macomber, a favorite author of mine, entitled, *One Simple Act – The Power of Generosity*. I bought it, read it, and smiled the whole time. It discusses how our lives can be enriched by being kind and generous. **It is not about the money!!** I can now tell you from personal experience when you make a spontaneous, generous gesture, it comes back to you in ways that you can never imagine. It is not about money, it has to do with kindness, gratitude, and many other things and it fills you with such joy that life begins to change for you.

When we are generous, our hearts expand and we want to be more generous. It has more to do with the heart and how we feel when we are sharing. It is rarely about money. Sometimes it is just about believing in someone, encouraging them, and helping them believe in themselves. Sometimes it can be something as simple as letting someone with two or three items go ahead of you in a check-out line or putting your thirteen cents of change in the plastic Humane Society doggie, smiling, leaving a generous tip -- the list goes on and on. It is about having a generous spirit, wanting to do good for others, helping someone else. It makes you feel so good you want to repeat the experience. It **always** comes back in some way from some direction, but that is not why you do it. You do it from a place of love and **that** is what makes it a heart-expanding experience.

Sometimes it is about the money and that's okay, too. There was an organization I had always wanted to send money to, but I had never felt I had the extra money to make a donation. Now that I seemed to have "extra" money to spend at the casino, I thought again about that five hundred dollar machine and my thoughts about that, so I just wrote out a check for the donation. I mailed it off and thought no more about it. It was about three months later when I received a check in the mail from a friend who had owed me some money. I loaned it knowing that I would probably never see it again. The check was made out for the full amount that she owed me and it was for about three times the amount of the donation I had mailed off months earlier. There was a time lapse, yes, but it came back, multiplied. When you are generous, it comes back to you. When you are kind, it comes back to you. It comes back sometime in some way, many times over. Debbie Macomber refers to it as the "Magic of Multiplication" and I think that pretty well sums it up.

In 2011, I volunteered with a nearby church to help with a Community Thanksgiving Dinner. This had been something the church had done for about twenty years. Food was prepared for eight hundred people that year. This is a dinner for anyone and everyone who wants to come in the city of Anderson and surrounding areas. I was asked to help supervise in the kitchen in 2012 and I was glad to help again. Food had once again been prepared for eight hundred. When I talked to Patty, the woman in charge, the next day she said that nine hundred forty-nine people had been served. The only food that we ran out of was dressing! I have no idea how we were able to feed one hundred forty-nine extra people, but I witnessed that happening. There is always enough. A spirit of thanksgiving, of gratitude, of service, of love as we do things for others allows for all needs to be fulfilled.

CHAPTER SEVEN

With Debbie Macomber's book fresh in my mind and Christmas around the corner, I knew I had a variety of options available on how to express generosity. Christmas is the time of the year when we have ample opportunities to be generous. I decided to do something really different, however. An idea began to emerge.

When I had moved to Anderson, I knew no one but Andrew, Amber, and the boys. It was shortly after I began losing weight that I occasionally would go out to eat at Panera – usually at breakfast. When you move, some people don't realize, and I was one of them, you are losing contact with any familiar face. I knew the clerks at the grocery, the mailman, and the people in my neighborhood when I lived in Vincennes. I knew people at the bank, ran into teachers, former students, etc. Everywhere I went I would see someone whose face I recognized even if I didn't actually "know" them by name. In Anderson I didn't see any familiar faces-- anywhere. At that time I was able to accept it because I had moved realizing I knew no one. I just didn't realize how isolated it would make me feel.

The folks at Panera were all so nice and friendly. I learned their names and they learned mine. Over the year or so that I had been going in, I got to know a bit about them and their families. They would greet me when I came in and I would chat with some of them. Panera had become my version of "Cheers"…" where everybody knows your name". I decided that I wanted to do something for everyone there. I set a figure in my head that I thought would cover what I had in mind and went to the casino to do some planning after lunch at Panera one Thursday afternoon.

I remember it was a Thursday afternoon because I was trying to gauge at that time if there was a luckier time to go and play: morning, afternoon, or evening. I don't think I ever came up with an answer to that, but I remember I had a fantastic time on that particular Thursday afternoon. I sat down at a machine I enjoyed playing. It was the only machine in a row of six that was unoccupied so that was where I landed. I rarely play a maximum bet on any machine, but I decided to that day. I put a twenty-dollar bill in and on the third hit, I went to a bonus round of twenty-five games, each of which paid three times what the normal spin would have paid. One of the spins gave me an additional twenty-five games. After the bonus was over I had over seven hundred dollars!!! I was thrilled. It was the first time I had won anything over fifty dollars at any one time.

There was a lady sitting to me, Flo, who was as excited watching this as I was. She had been winning too, so we sat and played and visited. Eventually the money got up over eight hundred dollars. I was enjoying the playing and visiting, so we continued to sit and visit and play. About two hours later, it was like a switch had been flipped to the "off" position. We both started losing what we had gained. I cashed out with a little over seven hundred dollars and left. I now had the money I needed to finance my Christmas surprise at Panera with some left over to give away elsewhere.

With the help of one of the managers that I called my Secret Elf, I ended up with a list of everyone who worked there. I had her get an idea of where they liked to eat out, hobbies, anything that could give me an idea for a gift. I got gift cards for restaurants, department stores, hardware stores, grocery stores, etc. I slipped them in a card with a thank-you note and signed it "Santa." I gave them to my "elf" one morning telling her again not to tell anyone who they were from. She didn't and it was great fun.

Part of the fun for me is to remain as anonymous as I can. I am finding that is not always easy. I think of generosity and the changes it sparked in my life and I would suggest that everyone try it and see what happens. It doesn't have to be any kind of financial expenditure. You can write a note to someone, send a card or note to a former teacher telling them how much they meant to you. You can pick up trash and put it in a trash can. Smile, smile, smile. The gift of a smile is a precious gift. You are taking time to get out of yourself, recognize someone else, and give of yourself to another. When you express your generous spirit in any way with no thought of getting anything in return, you are reaching a higher level of emotion and vibration in your life.

Expressing generosity, love, and kindness with no expectations contributes to the flow of all good things. You can look at nature and see the flow there. For example, water is in a constant state of change and movement. From rain soaking into the ground and evaporating into the atmosphere only to become rain again. It changes, depending on conditions, from solid to liquid, to gas, constantly changing forms yet always coming back. Water needs to be in a constant state of movement. If water sits, collects, and does not flow, it becomes murky and foul and stagnates. So too, with our spirit or soul. If we do not express ourselves in accordance with the flow of nature that we see around us, we experience stagnation and do not become all that we can be.

Seasons flow, all of life flows. You don't want to stop the flow. When you flow outward to others, sharing of yourself, from a generous spirit, that is what flows back to you. It was not coincidence or great luck that gave me the money at the casino when I needed it. It was the flow of generosity going out from me and coming back through me only to flow outward again. This flow is represented by a law that is referred to as the Law of Rhythm. This law states in its simplest form that everything flows and is cyclical in nature. There is a flowing out and back, much like a pendulum. This is working at all times. When you give thanks, expressing gratitude and appreciation for all you are asking, even before you get it, you are getting yourself into the flow of the never-ending stream of abundance. It is in the giving that you are expressing thanks for all that has flowed to you and through you. When you make a decision to be generous, don't second guess yourself. Be generous because that is who you are. In doing that, you are expressing thanks because you cannot give away that which you do not have and you are acknowledging the abundance in your life. Generosity is actually a thankful expression of all that you have received and been blessed with.

Sometimes we seem to dwell on the thought that we wonder if someone who is "deserving" will be the beneficiary of our gift. We are not giving to soothe our ego, we are giving to another. If we place a value on our judgment of another, the generosity will not flow. As I thought about this myself, I have often done that very thing and used it as an excuse not to give. I finally decided that if that same judgment of me had been given by others, there are many times I might have been deemed "undeserving." Again, don't second-guess a generous gesture, whether given or received, just be in the flow with appreciation.

CHAPTER EIGHT

We had an extremely mild winter that year and I found that I could get out and about much more easily than I had been able to during the previous two winters that I had lived up here. I spent time at the casino observing, thinking, socializing and just enjoying myself in general. Spring finally appeared and I was getting some cleaning and some gardening done. I was trying to find something interesting on television one evening when I came across a PBS special entitled, *Wishes Fulfilled* with Dr. Wayne Dyer. At that time I called Andrew to double check that it was, "the same guy who wrote *Excuses Begone!*" He assured me that it was, so I watched and recorded it.

There were two items that really caught my interest. He told us in that special that we are not our bodies and proceeded to show pictures of himself at various stages in life. I realized then that, indeed, I was not the same body I was at age 2 or 6 or 15 or 30. Every day cells in our body are being replaced with new cells. Our body works on literally recreating itself daily. Although we are a part of our body, our body itself is not who we really are. If it were, it would never change. He then stated that we need to ask ourselves, then, "Who am I?" As the special continued, I was mesmerized with the concept that by our thoughts, feelings, and attention to those, we could actually draw into our lives what we desired. He talked about changing our concepts of ourselves and stressed connecting with our highest self—our Source.

I listened to the special over and over. When I got rid of my cable connection and hence my DVR, I lost the presentation in the process but I had his book by then and had started absorbing a much more detailed account of manifesting. I will tell you right here and right now, the idea of having my wishes fulfilled was enticing. I love money!! I say that with no apologies. I like to spend money. I like to spend it on anyone and anything at any time. It is paper. It is a means to an end, something to be shared. I have never been concerned with saving a lot back. Some, yes, but I have never hoarded it. Sometimes in my life it has seemed that more has flowed out than in, but I have been very blessed in regards to the abundance in my life, and I know that. The idea that I could manifest wealth intrigued me. The more money I had, the more I could give away. I could also have more money to provide me with financial security in the future. Dr. Dyer had stated in his PBS presentation that the realizing of our wishes fulfilled is not as much about what we want as it is about who we are. It was not until much later that I understood the significance of that statement.

As I read his book, he suggested the *Tao te Ching* and *The Power of Awareness*, among others. I got all of those books and when another book was suggested, I got that also. I read book after book from April through September; some of them two or three times. As I read, my understanding of life around me began expanding. I started absorbing a much more detailed account of manifesting, of the Law of Attraction, and especially the importance of how we view life and live our lives. I began incorporating more and more of what I was learning into my life and my life was truly beginning to change.

It was about this time, in the spring, that Carolyn and I planned a casino junket to Biloxi, Mississippi. Glenda, her other sister, was going with us. Sandy was going to drive over from New Orleans and we were planning a fun-filled few days. Now, I don't know about everyone out there, but our partying days while in our sixties are not a whole lot different than they were in our twenties or thirties. None of us were ever wild, in the sense we think of "wild" in today's jargon. A great deal has changed since that time, and so has the definition of "partying" and "having a good time." We all grew up during the fifties and had been raised with a sense of respect that is much different than the way we raise our own kids. We had also been in our teens and early twenties during the unrest of the Vietnam War and all of the strife our country went through with demonstrations. The sixties was a time of the great Civil Rights Movement. Those two movements and events changed our country in much the same way that the destruction of the World Trade Center and resulting "war on terror" and the struggle for GLBT rights have. It shows us that perhaps we didn't learn the earlier lessons very well either. It has given us, as a people, a time to look at values and determine who we really are as members of the human race. It gives us time to look at our individual values and determine what ripples those decisions are sending out. But, I digress.

I had not reached the point in my reading that I was pursuing these deeper questions in life. I was just interested in the manifestation of wealth (which I translated to be "money") at that time. While we were there, Carolyn and Glenda went off to find the kind of machines that they enjoyed playing. Sandy and I preferred the penny slots so we sat together and played and visited and got to know each other pretty well. It was during some of these conversations that we discussed spiritual aspects of life. I told her about the manifesting that I had learned about through some of the books I had been reading. We discussed the meaning of wealth, abundance, prosperity, and decided that all of those terms encompass more than money. We have an abundance in our lives that transcends money. Money is only paper and it only has a value because we determine that it does. She then told me that she had a couple of books that she thought I might enjoy and we determined that she would send them to me. These were three books in a series by Neale Donald Walsch, entitled *Conversations with God.* The premise was that God had talked to this guy and he had basically transcribed the conversation they had. They sounded intriguing but I was skeptical that God would have an actual conversation with someone. How would that happen? If they would give me added insight to the deluge of new ideas, however, then I would read them too. Little did I realize where I was headed!

CHAPTER NINE

I have attempted to share enough about my life at this point to give you a frame of reference with which to see how my journey began to take off by leaps and bounds. I will share more of my background as I get to places where more clarification is needed. Part of this book has been very difficult for me to put into words. Many thoughts and feelings that I thought I had dealt with were really exposed to the light of my awakening and seen for what they were and dealt with in the realm of new understanding. It has provided a great healing for me. It has allowed me to escape much of the fear that I had lived with that had kept me from embracing who I really am. Our soul is constantly seeking to expand and this is really what this book is enabling me to do. I hope that it helps you question, seek, and find answers that will help you to realize the most wonderful life you can ever imagine.

When I moved to Anderson, I kept the duplex I owned where I had lived for twenty-seven years and raised my kids. It had been increasingly frustrating to be an absentee landlord so I decided the previous fall to put it on the market. There was finally had an interested party who made an offer and I accepted. She stalled on putting earnest money down and she was beginning to hedge on the price, finding other "things that need to be addressed." I was getting concerned about whether the sale was actually going to go through. It had not been shown since the offer was made, so I was losing valuable time if she didn't go ahead and buy it. A lease was coming up for renewal and I was going to have to rent it again and I thought a new landlord might rather make that decision, but I would not leave it empty waiting on her to make up her mind. I decided to apply what I had learned about manifesting and put it to use in this situation.

I called my realtor and left a message saying, "I am going to be in Vincennes on the twenty-third to close on the house." When I hung up the phone, **immediately, I knew** the house would be closing. I was excited. Thrilled!! I was meeting a friend in Indianapolis that day for lunch and told her that I was going down to Vincennes soon to close on the duplex. It never occurred to me that it would not happen. As I was driving home, I got a call from the realtor saying that the buyer was willing to drop any additional negotiations, that she had received a check for the earnest money, and had managed to get the closing set for the twenty-seventh if that would be okay. Okay?? It was great! The process worked amazingly fast in this instance. I have applied it since, and it has worked.

I want to say something here, about what happened with this. Yes, negotiations were already underway. Yes, it appeared that the sale would take place. Well, you say, that may just have been what was going to happen anyway. Yes, you are right, but so far it hadn't. That is the difference. We can be positive, we can wait, we can sit back and worry one way or the other, or we can actually project ourselves to the future and see it as we want it to be, and it will soon be. If this sale hadn't gone through, I saw myself so vividly closing on that house, it would have happened, maybe not the way it did, but some way. That is the magnificence of the law. When we can train our thoughts to believe and **feel** the outcome of our beliefs, it will come to fruition. The sale of the house manifested. Whether that was a result of a continual unfolding or whether it would have seemed to come from out of thin air, the manifestation of the desire was real and complete. The Law of Attraction will give to us the object of our focus.

After this experience, there was about a month I spent in reading daily for hours absorbing all the information I could from a variety of sources. I had found my attitude changing and my approach to life was becoming much different. I was reading many suggested titles from different authors that I found. Some of the different terminology kept me confused at times. One afternoon I was sitting on my deckio with my eyes closed, churning some of the thoughts over in my head wondering how I was going to keep it all straight so I could really apply it to my life. I heard someone say, "Why don't you write you own book?" My eyes popped open and I looked over at the back corner of the house. I was expecting to see someone, the voice was that vivid. There was no one. I thought about the entire experience and decided that the idea was a good one regardless of how it had come to me. I knew it was going to happen. (If you are reading this book, you know that it manifested in my life.)

The idea of writing a book was an entirely foreign concept to me and I had no idea where to start. I realized that I would need to do more than think and casually read. I was going to have to read more, and read with purpose. When I came to something interesting, I was going to actually have to research facts and follow where any information led me. I found myself getting involved in many different areas. When the physics of the Universe became a part of it, it morphed into more than I had every expected and it was even more and more unbelievable. But, all of the unbelievable parts about the Universe actually made all of the spiritual concepts more believable to me. If the unbelievable Universe exists then it is totally probable that all of the metaphysical aspects of it exist also.

I feel that now, because I will be writing a lot about thoughts and emotions involved in the whole process of my change, I need to address a couple of issues.

Number one - I am in **no way** making an attempt to present these concepts as original ideas. The amalgamation of thoughts are mine, but they stemmed from the writing and sharing of others and how my mind processed it. It is the story of my journey and quest. These are ideas and concepts from a variety of sources that I have incorporated while thinking and determining who I am. They represent my conscious awareness and the process and beliefs I have about who I am. It is simply the story of the path I am taking and how I got here. I am still learning, adjusting, incorporating, and reading. New ideas, concepts, and inspirations light my path daily. That is the great thing about our path--we may be headed into a thicket and decide to sit on a stump and ponder before we tackle it, or we may just decide to go around it rather than go through it. The journey is ours and we can do it in whatever way we want to. My path is different from anyone else's. My conscious path of awareness began at a casino in New Orleans and continued in Anderson, Indiana, but my journey began long before that.

Number two - While I find this path to be my path, I am not trying to convince anyone that it is the only path or the path they should take. There are many roads to any destination. If there is any wisdom or inspiration in my sharing which you can use in your journey, please take it up and add it to your thoughts and approach. We are all here on the planet together at this time to help and encourage each other. I believe we all have the desire to be loved, to be accepted for who we are and to be treated honestly and with respect. If, in my writing, I sound like I am being too vehement, please forgive me. I just have such a conviction about some of these ideas and issues that I tend to get a bit carried away. I believe we are all here to experience joy and happiness. If you get off the path for a while, do not worry, you will eventually find your way. There is no stopwatch on us as to how fast we need to reach our destination. Some authors will tell us that the journey is the joy, not the destination, and they may very well be right. The journey I believe is what is capable of helping us achieve the joy and happiness our soul longs for, if only we allow it to. We are an infinite spiritual being in a finite physical body for a brief period of time, meant to enjoy the experience.

CHAPTER TEN

If you ask anyone what they would like in life, those answers will usually revolve around money, or something that money can buy. Some of the answers you might receive would range from: new house, renovation of the house I have, summer cottage, more money in the bank, bigger house, better job, better car, new car, money for kid's college education, money for vacations, etc. You would also hear things like happiness, peace, and contentment.

The first items are the desires of our ego. We often want what we perceive that we are lacking in order to impress others, or to prove to ourselves that we are successful. Many times we strive for something we don't have, that we think we need to make us happy or content. When we get whatever it is, we find that we are still not happy. Then we think of something else that we are certain will make us happy. When we get that, we still aren't happy. The ego is always trying to get more, achieve more, it strives for what it leads us to believe we must have. There is nothing wrong about wanting any of the material things in our life that we desire. The problems occur when we think that "things" will make us happy, will give us joy, or will fulfill us in any way. Where you live, what kind of car you drive, and how much money you have in the bank means very little if you exist in a state of constant dissatisfaction with your life.

The latter part of the list are things that the soul desires, things that the very essence of our being desires. These are the things that a house, a car, money, or a better job will never satisfy. If we go after the desires of the soul by putting the ego out of the way, we will gain our happiness, peace, and contentment. Those qualities and desires of the soul can only be reached when we give to others through kindness, generosity, and compassion. When we give of ourselves in that way, the needs of the soul are met and we are joyous. We come to realize that the only thing we need to have a happy life is to **be** happy. When we are able to put the "things" in life in the proper perspective, our need to keep acquiring "stuff" disappears because our soul is fulfilled. Then, the most amazing thing occurs. When our soul is fulfilled, we begin to manifest the objects of our desire.

`Many, many people of all walks of life will be quick to agree that they were happier when they were young and starting out in life. They didn't have a lot of "things." They were satisfied with handed down furniture, lumpy couches, a table with two chairs, stacked milk crates for storage. As they achieved more in life, they began wanting more and they became dissatisfied when they couldn't get what they wanted. "All of a sudden", the second hand car wasn't good enough. Furniture purchased new three years ago didn't go with the new color scheme for the bedroom, so new furniture had to be purchased. Time after time, what a person was thankful for when they got it, no longer seemed to satisfy. Newer and better had to be achieved, in all areas. It escaped into the people in your life—the old tried and true friends were suddenly not good enough. The husband didn't make enough money, so you looked for a new one. The wife got a bit older so you looked for one younger. This is the way the ego leads people over and over again. It happens this way and for those reasons.

Ponder upon these things for a bit and see where your thoughts take you.

1. What would I like to have in my life materially? Why?
2. Am I satisfied with my life on most days?

3. Are there areas of my life that I am dissatisfied with. What are they, and what do I think would make it better? And why do I think that would make it better

4. Do I let the weather, other people's opinions, or news reports affect my state of either well-being or unrest?

5. When do I feel the happiest and really enjoy my days?

CHAPTER ELEVEN

There are two very powerful bits of information that I came across time and time again in my reading. The first was the Law of Attraction and the second was the two most powerful words in the world. I am introducing them here because I will be referring to them and explaining them in more depth as they unfolded in my experience. Just becoming aware of them was the first step.

There is said to be a universal Law of Correspondence that is powered by your thoughts, feelings, and convictions. Within this law is the Law of Attraction which is always working and drawing to us that to which we give our focus. The Law of Attraction very simply states that we are constantly attracting things in our life to us as a result of our thoughts, feelings, and attention. Whatever we believe to be true about ourselves is what we will attract to us until our thoughts and feelings about ourselves change. When our thoughts and feelings change, we will begin attracting different things to us accordingly. We will attract either that which we want, or that which we don't want, depending on where our thoughts are focused. When you combine the Law of Attraction with the two most powerful words in the universe, you become the co-creator in drawing to you a life of your conscious choosing. Those two words? **"I am."**

When you use the words, "I am" you are aligning or partnering yourself with the God of your understanding. What will come to pass depends on what follows these two words. These words have the power they have because they were the way in which God first revealed himself to humankind through Moses in the Bible. This revelation crosses religious boundaries for a complete explanation because it was through translations in the Talmud that this first became apparent. James Twyman explains the story and its significance fully in his book, *The Moses Code*. *The Moses Code* is about the realization that we are all one with God and once we realize that, we can act with the power and passion of God in the world. For those who think this is an outlandish statement, Jesus, himself, told us in the New Testament, "Ye are Gods." He also said in John 14:12, "Truly, truly, I say to you, he who believes in me (flesh and blood, as are you), the works I do he shall do also, and greater works than these shall he do." The miracles or manifestations that occur in your life are called upon by you; they are not, however, produced by you. It doesn't matter whether the miracle is small or large. God will give you what you ask for and what you believe will appear.

"I am" is something we say all the time. If we follow these words negatively, we will attract negativity and things will not go well for us. If we follow them with words that reflect an alignment with the positive, then positive things will be drawn to us. We are always **I am**. Which will it be," I am sick," "I am healthy," "I am weak," or " I am strong"? Whatever we say will align us with that which we express, that which we feel, and the vibration and emotion associated with it. Keep in mind that the feelings we have about these statements are extremely important. We cannot just state something like, "I am kind," if we cannot feel and act in a kind manner, in other words if we cannot **be** kind.

Some things that will help you assimilate the "I am" aspect of you into your life:

1. Become aware of how many times you use the phrase, "I am"... is it followed by something positive (I am so happy) or something negative, (I am sick and tired of this)?

2. What would you have in your life, do in your life, or be in your life that you don't already have?

3. Begin taking the positive "I am "statements and say them aloud when you wake up and before you go to sleep. One of the best ones is, "I am thankful" and **feel** thankful as you are saying it. Think of family, friends, everything in your life, flowers, blue sky, rain, sun, butterflies, whatever you can include in your gratitude. Feel gratitude for all that is given to your, whether you perceive it as good or bad... be thankful at all times for all things.

4. Continue to look at life and everything that encompasses it and concentrate on what you have rather than what you feel might be missing. Continue to feel thankful and blessed for all you have. The more gratitude you can express, the more you will find appearing in your life for which to give even more thanks.

CHAPTER TWELVE

I spent the first sixty years of my life in a state of grumpiness. I am happy to say that I am no longer a grumpy person. I still have my grumpy moments, but I find that I look forward to every day. No day is without its challenges, but they no longer affect me in the same way. I still get aggravated, I still get irritated, but the episodes are fewer and farther between and shorter in scope. I do not let those times define me. It is a real transformation in my life. I am feeling that change from within. If it can happen for me, I know that it can happen for anyone. It is a matter of aligning ourselves with our highest self and a higher power or Source energy. I refer to that Source as "God", but use whatever the Source of your understanding is. I am not sure you even have to give this energy and light within you a name. If you allow yourself to feel the magnificence of the world around you, you will tap into that source of energy and vibration that just "is."

We cannot wait for external experiences to make us happy, content, or peaceful. Those qualities will never be found externally. I spent years looking for "things" to make me happy; they were not to be found. We have to **be** happy, **be** content, and **be** peaceful. I was very skeptical about this whole process but decided I had nothing to lose and everything to gain on the "off chance" that it would do something to help me spend less time mired in negativity. No one could ever have convinced me that my life could change so dramatically.

I will often use Biblical quotes to illustrate a point, but this is not a theological book. I am not a Bible scholar by any stretch; nor, am I even a student of the Bible. My reading is much more secular and spiritual than religious. I will draw from ancient wisdom of Lao Tzu in the *Tao te Ching*. I will use examples we have seen during our lifetime of the Dalai Lama. I will use quotes to emphasize points from a wide range of sources, usually because as I have been trying to think of something to illustrate a point, I have run across a quote that does it much more accurately.

I am a Christian, Protestant, Methodist, but I am not an elitist that believes Christianity is the only way to know God, it is just one way. What I say comes from a Christian frame of reference, but is probably more Universalist in concept. These are merely thoughts of mine. Questions I have had, paths I have traversed to get me to where I am now. I do not view them as right or wrong, they merely are what they are, as are your beliefs. They express a lot about me in my previous years, and how I reached the place I had, how I began thinking, how it changed my thinking, and how it is changing my life. This book comes from an understanding of only about a year. None of us can be hurried along our path, and this is as it should be.

Thoughts…hmm…what are they and where do they come from? If you "think" about it, we don't really think. Of course, there are those times in life, like when we are in school, that we consciously direct our minds in a direction it needs to go and concentrate our thoughts on a specific subject, but I am talking about the process of thinking itself. Random thoughts just seem to appear without any effort on our part. There are estimates that indicate that we have about sixty thousand thoughts cross our mind every day. If we are studying and concentrating on something, we can focus those thoughts. Our minds usually seem to be chaotic. Although we can't stop the flow of thoughts, we can choose which thoughts we are going to give our attention to. In this way, we can develop an awareness of the kind of thoughts we are having. All of this sounds kind of circular. Sometimes it does to me too, but it will circle back and fall in place. Several of the books I read, as I decided I needed to research some specific ideas, addressed the importance of our thoughts. After we have a thought, our emotions and feelings will act on it. As we become aware of the kinds of thoughts we are having, we can choose which thoughts we accept, and which ones we just let go on by and don't dwell on. Because the Law of Attraction is always at work, drawing to us that which we think about, good or bad, our thoughts become even more important.

Let's say we get up one morning, it is rainy and when we move we have some achiness in our joints. Our thoughts about these two situations can make the experience of our day totally different. We can choose to think about the rain and how we don't like gloomy days. Then we decide we don't want to get up, we're still tried because rainy mornings zap our strength and make us feel like staying in bed. We begin to think of all the things that we had hoped to do in the yard and get aggravated that we will have to do them another day. Then there is the problem that rainy days cause us to have with our back and knees. Yep, sure enough, we're experiencing some pain. We decide we had better take some medication so the pain will get better; otherwise, we remind ourselves, it is sure to get worse.

The person next door wakes up to the very same rainy day and also has some achiness in their joints. They stretch out while still in bed and notice the achiness but don't dwell on it or on their stiff knees. They lay there and just give themselves a few minutes to enjoy listening to the sound of the rain. It occurs to them that since it is raining, they can't mow the yard so they will have time to start a different project that will be perfect for a rainy day. Maybe they can treat themselves to a day of reading. They get up and go about their day, knowing the achy joints will work themselves out, they usually do, and if they don't then they will deal with that when it occurs.

Changing experiences in life can truly be that simple, when we allow it to **be**. We cannot change the fact that it is raining, period. When we choose our thoughts we can change our experience of the event; hence, changing the reality of the event. The rainy day can be either something we gripe about, or something we look at as a chance to do something that a rainy day is perfect for doing. The thoughts and feelings that we hold on to will draw those very things into our experience. When we can practice (and it does take practice to make it become natural) consciously choosing our thoughts about how we will experience the events around us, we will notice our life changing. In this case, it will be a disgruntled experience, or a creative experience, depending on our thoughts, feelings, and actions. Our reality in this situation can be one of frustration or one of anticipation.

When we make a conscious decision to be responsible for the thoughts we dwell on, we can influence what is attracted to us in the future. If we dwell on what we don't want, then what we don't want will be attracted to us. There was a phrase I read, attributed to Carl Jung, "What you resist, persists." In other words, rather than dwell on a negative, which will be giving it attention and therefore causing it to persist, let it be one of the thoughts that you put on a conveyor belt in your mind and get it carried out of your stream of consciousness.

There is a history of cancer in my family and I am a cancer survivor myself. I used to always say that "cancer will be what gets me." I no longer say that. There has been a great deal of cellular research done by Bruce Lipton, PhD. which he shared in his book, *The Biology of Belief.* His research indicates that conscious thought can override genetic information that was previously thought to control aspects of our health. If I understood the information correctly, each and every cell in our bodies has a consciousness, an intelligence, which our thoughts influence. If we combine this research with the Law of Attraction which gives us what we focus on, it becomes our responsibility to focus on health rather than disease and sickness. If I focus on cancer—which I don't want—I could actually be sending my cells messages that would attract it to me. Diseases are merely a dis-ease of the body. Now, I focus on being healthy by telling myself with conviction and belief that I am healthy. I also become more aware of my eating habits by including as many fresh fruits and vegetables as possible. I avoid processed foods whenever I can. The closer I eat foods in their natural state, I know the healthier I will be. Once again, my thoughts influence my actions and together they influence my experience.

I don't waste time stressing over much anymore, because I know that whatever I am giving my attention to is what I will attract. Do I still have negative and unproductive thoughts? You betcha! It would probably be impossible not to, considering those sixty thousand thoughts that come streaming through our minds uninvited. I dismiss them as soon as I realize they have paused for a time; and, I then put calm positive thoughts in their place. I don't think about those negative thoughts either because that would be giving them attention and power. I dismiss the negativity and send the thoughts on their way. Sometimes this is not easy, the thoughts and negativity keep creeping back in. Don't beat yourself up when that happens and don't dwell on it. It takes practice, and sometimes very concentrated effort to just bless the thoughts and put them on the conveyor belt to go far, far away.

I have found that there are things that help me do this. I no longer watch news because of the negativity that is produced for me. I don't miss the drama, negativity, violence, and noise that television seems to produce. I will listen to music that moves me – sometimes that is classical, sometimes The Mills Brothers, and sometimes Little Richard!! Sometimes just taking a good book out on the deckio with a glass of peach tea and spending a very quiet evening will renew my spirit. Maybe you feel that peace when you take your dog for a walk, go running or go to a Zumba class. Maybe digging in the garden is what relieves tensions and gives you time to connect with your higher self. That is really what it is all about, replacing the irritated feelings with positive feelings. The feelings we have about everything are one of the keys. When we do get irritated, let it go, don't continue to be irritated, or let it lead to something else irritating you even more. If you are able to neutralize the original irritation, let yourself become aware of what is happening, and shift away from the irritation, you will become more and more aware. Awareness of how we react to every event we experience is another one of the keys if we are to be successful in making positive changes in our lives.

CHAPTER THIRTEEN

As I read more, I sensed a greater value of the "spiritual" over "organized religion" in the authors' writings. It was not stated as such by the authors; but, it was rather a feeling that I began to sense from within. There seemed to be themes of tolerance leading to acceptance as well as unity and oneness. This is something that we don't hear much about in many of our organized churches. I thought about this and as I read suggested books, I began to feel that sense of unity with Source (or God) and the oneness with everyone became more apparent in my views and my actions. I was beginning to question many previous teachings because I was becoming aware that many of those teachings didn't really reflect my own thoughts and beliefs. They had been handed to me by various churches at various times in my life. I had not questioned them, I had just accepted them as being the way a Christian was supposed to think.

I have always had a difficult time when I have stopped to think of Heaven and Hell. Religion teaches us that God is love. God is good, but unless we (in the Christian religion) confess our sins and accept Jesus as our Savior who died on the cross for our sins, before we die, we not only would never get to Heaven but would also suffer never-ending torment in a place called Hell. We seem to be instructed that not only do we have to believe this, but it is our duty to go out and spread the word and get everybody else to believe this way also. I always wondered where all of the people who predated

Jesus figured into this equation. Does that mean that Moses went to Hell? I wondered where the faithful Jews, American Indians, Buddhists, and other devout people would end up. It just never did make any sense to me. If God is love, would he put us here then set up a list of do's and don'ts waiting for us to screw up then condemn us forever? I personally don't think so.

It was when I read the book, *If Grace is True,* written by Philip Gulley and James Mulholland that I was able to put the pieces of the puzzle in place for me. We get reunited with God by grace. To paraphrase Gulley and Mulholland, God is like the father of the Prodigal Son in the Bible. He sees us and has compassion and love for us. He welcomes us home. (I will be using the masculine pronouns to refer to God, or Source energy, but as you will see later, gender is something humans have created, there is no gender to God.) Grace is not a reward that can be earned; nor, is it a gift, given to some and withheld from others. According to Gulley and Mulholland, "Grace is God's unfailing commitment to love." Salvation means being freed of every obstacle to intimacy with God. Using "salvation" in these terms means we no longer have to fear the wrath of God, we can just be free to accept the love that is offered.

Most people believe in a god-power of some kind in some way. I don't believe that when all is said and done in this physical life of ours that it will make any difference to the Source of creation whether we have been Christian, Buddhist, or Atheist. I think of an Atheist as a free thinker who has opted against organized religion. I think they are bravely forging their own path as we all are, and are honest enough to admit that they don't have all of the answers. Some that I have encountered are, however, as zealous in their lack of belief in "God" as some Christians are in their worship of Jesus. I have known people who claim to be Atheists who have exhibited more "God-like" qualities like kindness, compassion, and generosity than some Christians I have known – including myself, at times in my life.

Churches quite often seem to put up more barriers to God than necessary. We are said to be created in the image of God, but I think we have turned that around and given God human characteristics. We can encounter God's grace when we are on a beach watching the tide come in, when we lay on the ground and look at the clouds drifting by, or when we hold a baby. God fills our everyday activities with many opportunities to experience His magnificence. We don't have to be in a church to feel God's presence or His love. God doesn't have to appear in a burning bush, as He did with Moses, but He most assuredly will be a light in our life. Most often we can experience Him in the soft breezes that cool us in the summer or in the stars that we observe in the night sky. We experience His grace and love daily in the air we breathe, the sun that shines on us, and in all of nature. If God's grace is true, then (as Gulley and Mulholland tell us) it is true for everyone, not just a chosen few.

Jesus is the representative of God that Christians recognize and Deify. Jesus is but one path to God. There are many paths, as represented by different religions, scriptures, and beliefs. What I found interesting as I was researching is that in Islam, Jesus is recognized as one of God's highest ranked and most beloved prophets. Jesus didn't turn away from anyone. He was stoned, ridiculed, outcast, yet he knew what we spend a lifetime trying to find – Peace during strife, Joy in the mundane, and Hope in times of tragedy. Jesus's life was full of situations that would cause any human to suffer, complain, judge, and gripe. Jesus turned from all of it to display the "God-power" of his flesh. We must remember, if anything makes any sense to us at all, that Jesus was a human, flesh and blood, just like we are. What Jesus possessed that set him apart was the knowledge that he was part of God, he was God, and he behaved as God would behave if He had a physical body. I think that is what I am doing here, what my purpose is, what we are all doing here. We are all called on to **be** God in the flesh. Jesus, himself, told us, "Ye are Gods." He also told us, "What I can do, you can do also, these things and even more."

There are a couple of books that give credence to the God-power in each of us. *The Biology of Belief* and *The God Code* deal directly with physical evidence that support our oneness with God. Cellular research was conducted by Bruce Lipton, PhD, over his lifetime that he shares in his book, *The Biology of Belief*. In his research, he discovered that each cell exhibits the intelligence that is mirrored in multi-cellular organisms. It is an intelligence that surpasses DNA coding. Our cells can operate independently of DNA, depending on what thoughts, feelings, and convictions we consciously send to them. It is when they work collectively that they are able to perform the processes needed for their survival (of respiration, digestion, etc.) indicating oneness in purpose. When you combine this information with Gregg Braden's research in *The God Code,* you find that numerically verified coding in our cells prove that the name of God (translated from both Hebrew and Aramaic texts of religious scripture) are the same as the elements of hydrogen, nitrogen, oxygen, and carbon that are part of each living cell of every living organism on the planet. When our religious teachings instruct us to "look within" it becomes a directive that the truth of our oneness with God is literally stamped upon every one of the cells in our body. "Do unto others as you would have others do unto you" then takes on a more personal meaning. We are literally one with God; we are all the embodiment of God. God cannot be divided and made anything less than what He is. For each of us to be made in the image of God means that we are one with Him and with every living thing on the planet.

Jesus did not come to start a religion. He was born as any other baby, as we are all with earthly parents and the essence of God. He cried and he played as all our children do. We have been led to believe that Jesus was perfect. He was, and so are we all. God does not create imperfection. How could He, when He is all that was, is, or ever will be? Since He cannot be divided and made less than one, how could part of what cannot be divided, be less than what is? God does not make the judgments that mankind does. After all, what does perfect mean? What is perfect to each individual is a reflection of their own lives. What I call perfect, you may call unacceptable, much less than perfect. What would happen if we acknowledge that everything that goes on around us is perfect, not placing any judgment on it, just allowing it to exist without assessing it? To God, we are all perfect. We are part of His energy, regardless of what we are doing and how we are living our lives because He knows who we really are. We are not our bodies and we are not our actions. We are pure spirit and it is one with Him and with all others. We have given this spirit a name – our soul. He knows this, even if we have forgotten. He loves us all, cares for us all, and gives abundantly to us all. It is when we impose our restrictions and values on the planet and each other that we experience that which we call imperfect.

God doesn't limit His love to just a few people. He doesn't restrict His communication to just the Christian Bible. He doesn't single out any religion as special. God is not religious. He speaks to all people in every way at all times, even when we choose not to listen. Miracles still happen every day. We often don't recognize them because we have a preconceived idea of what it would take for something to be considered a miracle. What would happen to our life if you were able to view **everything** as miraculous? Give thanks for all you experience, good and bad, and your life will change. I can say this because that is what happened in my life and what is still happening as my life is unfolding. I can verify that miracles do still happen—to all of us.

I am experiencing a life of wonder and excitement. You can too. Change your thoughts, your approach to life situations, and your life will indeed change. God speaks to all people at all times in all ways. He speaks through the scriptures of all religions. None of them are the only word of God but all of them are the word of God. You don't need to believe in God to believe in yourself. When you believe in yourself, you are believing in God because you are one with Him. God does not need our worship or our acknowledgement, simply because He **is** God. Human ego thinks that because it constantly seeks approval from others that God operates this way also. Why would God need proof of his magnificence? He doesn't. God speaks to us in the silence, in the sunsets, in the blizzard, in the bloom of a violet. God is everywhere. If we only have the "eyes to see and the ears to hear." Most religions hold up their set of scriptures as being the one and only ultimate word of God. We limit God's communications with us when we do that. Rather than bringing us to oneness and unity with each other and our Source, we become divided and separated from Him and each other. God cannot be divided. It is the awakening of your soul that will ultimate set you free from unhappiness and fear.

CHAPTER FOURTEEN

There was in the beginning, God, a magnificent energy. For God to experience Himself, expansion into "something else" had to happen. I can certainly imagine that with this energy and magnificence, it would not be inappropriate to refer to it as a "Big Bang." Since God can't be divided into anything less than He is, everything created was also all of Him. In this expansion, all that ever was, is, or ever will be was created. **It is all God.** Dark and light, up and down, here, there, nowhere, everywhere, and all the space in between. In this expansion, creation took place.

The only thing that is happening now is the manifestation of all. Manifestation is thought that happens in our world. By conscious awareness, we direct our thoughts and manifest in our lives what we attract. Thoughts are creating our world as we experience it. If our thoughts are only of good, then only good will become our experience. Everything unfolds in Divine order and Divine time. All time is only relative. Yesterday was today when it was happening. Tomorrow will be today when we get there. Our past (let's use our sixth birthday as an example) occurred in the now, as the present. Only after we go through many other "now's" does that particular "now" become our "past." All we have – ever-is "now," "today," "this moment." Our "tomorrows" are rooted in our thoughts today.

This book has times when the thoughts expressed seem to drift off and then will circle back. This is partly by design and partly because that is the nature of life and an illustration of the Law of Rhythm. When discussing some of the Universal Laws, keep in mind they are called this because they describe the way the universe seems to be working. There are spiritual laws and physical laws and, for the most part, we will be referring to the spiritual laws of the universe (though concepts often overlap somewhat.) The Law of Attraction is one of the spiritual laws that is always working. It works in both the physical and spiritual realms. If you attract what you desire in the material world without considering the emotional and spiritual aspect of your life, you may find that what you attract doesn't satisfy you. I am sharing ideas and thoughts that came to me that I couldn't ignore. The more I understood, the more I wanted to know. There is no timetable because it is all happening now. Your consciousness and understanding of all of these concepts will occur for you when the time is right, and it will be in your "now" moments.

I used to grow herbs and had a small business I ran from my home. I had a plant, Sweet Annie, which I would gather and sell in the fall for dried arrangements. It was an annual which means it started fresh from seed every year. It dropped miniscule seeds by the millions and plants would pop up everywhere in the spring of the following year. I would pull plants up all the time and after about five years I decided I no longer wanted that particular plant in my garden. Even though I pulled it all up one year, I kept getting stray seedlings for about three or four years. Wherever I disturbed soil I uncovered some of the seeds and the growing conditions were just right for them to germinate. I had forgotten about this plant until I moved some plants from Vincennes to Anderson. I now have Sweet Annie again. Seeds can be there but until conditions are right, the plant will not grow. So it is with new ideas and concepts. We may hear some of them, file them away, and not give them another conscious thought. Suddenly, or so it seems, someone says something, or you see a movie, or hear a piece of music that triggers the memory of this new idea. You reflect on it from a different perspective of different experiences and it may "take root." Sometimes, just like my Sweet Annie, this takes years for the seed of a new idea to germinate, but it will when the conditions are right, if it is meant to be a part of your experience of reality.

CHAPTER FIFTEEN

Love is all there is. The Bible, and many other scriptures and pieces of wisdom address love. The Bible tell us that love is patient and kind. It is not jealous or boastful. Love bears all things, knows all things and endures all things. This is not the kind of love we usually embrace. When we express love, we often put demands and conditions on the other person in the relationship. These demands, unstated naturally, require that they behave in certain ways in order for us to continue to love them. All the while they are putting their unstated constraints on us. We withhold ourselves hoping that we can be a recipient of another's love or friendship We try to anticipate what we think that they want and try to be that kind of person. We are afraid to speak up and speak out about what our needs are and what we have to offer them in the relationship. When time passes and we decide to be ourselves, our true selves, they think we have changed. Likewise we do the same to them. Love, pure, true love, gives others freedom. When you truly love all others, as you would yourself, you do not put any expectations on them. When you come from a place of love for them, they will not disappoint you. They will not feel compelled to act in a certain way to gain your love, they have it and they give it back to you. (I am not speaking in this description of love as being romantic love, hence the difficulty when we only have one word for love of all kinds.)

When we read some of the descriptions of love in the Bible, some people choose to say this means that when someone is abusive, we need to bear it, stay in a relationship, and endure the abuse. This is not what love is, nor is that what is meant. We need to learn to love ourselves. When we love ourselves, we will see that abuse is not in any way, something that has to be endured, because abuse is not an expression of love. When we accept the unity of us all in spirit, we will want for others what we want for ourselves. When we love in a relationship of any kind, it should not be to see how our needs can be met. We will show to others that which we would like to receive and we will receive it from some source. Love given to others freely comes back to us many time over from some direction.

Love frees our soul or spirit. When our soul is free, we are joyous, we can respond in no other way because joy is the language of the soul. It is our nature to be joyous but our ego restrains us because we become afraid of losing love if we express it too deeply. We are afraid we will be hurt, and often we will, if that is how we choose to perceive it. We allow ourselves to be afraid of love, and hence life. This I know all too well. I absorbed messages that gave me love with conditions. If I argued or disagreed, it was a reason not to be loved. If I didn't look or act in a certain way, it was a reason to be denied love. I was given messages of conditional love my entire life, and the idea of anyone, even me, loving myself was not a possibility. Until it was. When you believe in the oneness of us all you will be able to look at everyone you come into contact with and see yourself in them and will love them. What we see in others is merely a reflection of ourselves. If we cannot love others, it is because we cannot love ourselves, warts and all. If we judge others, it is because we are judging ourselves. We project onto others what we cannot accept about ourselves and figure that if we can't tolerate our own flaws that no one else will be able to either. This is where kindness, generosity, and compassion come into play. Be as kind, as generously accepting, and as compassionate with yourself as you need to be. We are perfect, just as we are. There are no mistakes in God's eyes. When we can accept the perfection that is in us, we can accept the perfection in others and our world will indeed change.

CHAPTER SIXTEEN

For the next bit of discussion it will be helpful to address a little physics. All matter is energy, only energy. We are energy vibrating. Energy at different frequencies vibrates differently. Frequency, simply put, means how often (how quickly) the vibrations are occurring. In the book, *Ask and It is Given,* by Esther and Jerry Hicks, there is a list of emotions that help us gauge our connection to Source energy. The highest positive emotions of joy, freedom, love and appreciation are said to vibrate at a higher frequency (faster) than the lower negative emotions of worry, anger, and fear. Among other things you learn in this book, is the ability to get emotionally from where you are to a better emotionally vibrating place. While we may not be able to jump directly from despair to joy, we can work our way from despair to something higher on the list. We may be starting at disappointment and go to frustration, on up to boredom, then to hopefulness, and so on. It is not always a quick process, but it is a way in which we can improve how we are feeling about what we are experiencing. The ultimate goal is to connect to the feelings of joy and love which are the most closely connected to our Source energy. Eventually, we will get to the feelings of joy, love, and appreciation that are so necessary if we are to live a fulfilling life.

How helpful this list and these suggestions and activities would have been for me in life. I spent the first sixty years of my life in insecurity, guilt, unworthiness, anger, doubt, worry, and disappointment – all in the bottom half of the Hicks' list. Most of the time, pessimism was a high as I got with occasional bouts of enthusiasm. I felt that I was incapable of happiness and joy, incapable of loving or being loved. My marriage did very little to change those feelings. I was always afraid that I would say the wrong thing or do the wrong things and my husband would quit loving me. It wasn't that I did not express my feelings and ideas in the marriage, I did. If I was upset, I let it show. The more isolated I felt in the relationship, the more sharp-tongued I became. Our marriage deteriorated and communication became almost non-existent, unless my one-sided ranting counted. I knew that I had pushed the limits of his endurance and that he knew that I was not someone who could be loved. It turned out that he didn't quit loving me but he had his own path to follow and it didn't include me.

I discovered shortly after our eighth anniversary that my husband was gay. I cannot, even after thirty years, describe the emotions I felt when I learned this. To say that the world dropped out from under me would be an understatement. I experienced disbelief, shame, anger and hatred, the like of which I had never felt before (or since), and revenge was also high on my list of emotions. The one thing I did get was a release from guilt that I had not been able to make the marriage work. I knew then and there that I would never marry again. I decided that to never go through another divorce, the only way to insure that was to never have another marriage. What transpired was not pretty, it was not healthy, it was not productive, but it was what it was.

I read everything I could about homosexuality and got little from it. This happened in 1981. It happened at a time when you did not hear about "normal" people being "gay." We actually had one friend who was gay, everyone accepted it, but it was never discussed. He was unique and a bit flamboyant, but we all enjoyed his sense of humor and it was not an issue. He brought no "boyfriend" around and just joined in with the rest of us when we all got together. Obviously, my husband was closeted so I really have no idea if there were others that we ran with were gay and still have not "come out of the closet." It would not have mattered; I just didn't adjust well to having my life turned upside down by marriage to a gay man. I remember that one thing I did think at the time was that if gay men and women were not ostracized by society they would not need to try to "fit in" to a heterosexually-oriented world by marrying someone of the opposite sex. (I find this to be the most compelling reason our states and government need to grant marriage equality. If a gay person is given equal rights under the law, they will no longer need to hide who they are behind a heterosexual façade. It may still not be accepted by some people, but they cannot be discriminated against legally by anyone.) I knew it had nothing to do with me. It was evidently something that could not be explained, nor could it be changed; no more than heterosexuality can be explained or changed. I determined that he would never have left his children and ventured into a world of judgment and rejection had there been an alternative for him.

He was and still is a good father. I recognized that at the time, but I did not want his lifestyle messing with **my** kids. I was afraid that he could influence "gayness" in the kids, even though with all the reading on the subject that I had done, I knew this was not the case. I didn't want him to have his gay friends around the kids when he had visitation. He was granted visitation once a month and he got the kids when the court said he could. I seldom granted any additional time for them to spend with him. I worked with him on holidays, but I wasn't happy about it. I made it my mission in life to heap as much guilt and misery on him as I could. I was bitter, mean, callous and nasty. There has not been a word invented that I have not said to him. Every cruel and hateful word used against gays has come from my lips. When I hear all of the conservative political comments, it is an echo of everything I expressed to him thirty years ago. I pulled the God card, the
Bible card, every card that could be pulled, I did it and I said it. I wanted him to suffer, with a capital "S." I felt betrayed, unloved, frustrated, overwhelmed, miserable, hateful and vicious. It was the worst time in my life. I was going to make certain I would never get myself in a position to feel that hurt again. I would never love anyone again. What I did not begin to understand at the time was that what I was doing to him was coming back at me many times over. I thought that everything that was happening was being done

to me. All of the time that this was happening, I didn't think that there was anything wrong with this behavior, after all, I had been wronged!!

CHAPTER SEVENTEEN

Jump ahead twenty-five years. Our thirty-year-old daughter, Allison, decided her biological clock was ticking down. In her teens, Allison had decided she did not want to marry and have children. She had some physical concerns in her early twenties that might have taken that choice away from her. A few years later she told me she might like to have kids someday, but not to expect her to get married. While there is much of this story that is shared elsewhere, she had a daughter when she was thirty years old. I had bonded with this baby before birth. I had seen her turn her face and smile at me on the first ultra-sound. When Allison called to tell me that Cheyenne had been born, I was told to stay away from the hospital. How could this be? Once again, the story behind the story is not a pleasant one and will be shared later. What I am going to share right now is that Don was instrumental in getting Allison to let me see Cheyenne. He worked at it from the time Cheyenne was born. Allison would call and talk, and I would ask questions about my granddaughter. I would ask to see her and Allison would just tell me, "not yet."

The first time I held my grand-daughter was at a Border's bookstore when she was three months old. Here again, it is difficult for me to express how I felt. Someone who knew the heartache of not being able to be with children he loved helped the woman who tried to keep him from those children. He knew the pain yet he wanted to help me. He didn't want me to keep experiencing that kind of pain. This speaks of his character, the character he had always possessed, and it is something that can't be ignored for any reason. This is an example of grace in action. He was being who he is and that was all he was doing thirty years ago. He could have sat back and thought, "serves you right, Bitch," but he didn't. That is not who he is. It never was. He exhibited unbelievable kindness. It gave me a great deal of healing. I got to that place where I was able to truly, deeply forgive what I had perceived as transgressions toward me; and, in that action, I was able to forgive myself. I have recently expressed to him how much I appreciated what he did for me and let him know how very sorry I am for all the unkind things that I had done years earlier. I apologized for my actions. Yet again, with kindness, he let me know that it was no longer something for me to beat myself up about, that we had gotten through it. I feel we are friends now and I look forward to sharing family experiences with him.

If you are struggling with this issue in your family, I do understand. One thing that I will say it this, "it is an issue only for as long as you choose to make it an issue." I am going to ask you to do something, for your sake and the sake of your gay family member or friend. Embrace them and tell them you love them for the person they are, just as they are. You don't need to understand anything at all about homosexuality, just be kind and accepting of **them.** Apply the Golden Rule and treat them as you would want others to treat you if you were in that situation. Pulling out the Bible card, the religion card, or any argument you have at all is not productive. It does nothing to help the situation, their ability to deal with it, or your ability to accept it. They do not suddenly become a different person. They are still your friend, your brother, your sister, your child, or your parent. They have won't morphed into some kind of monster to be feared. Acceptance is one of the greatest gifts we can give to anyone, because it is a gift of love.

If you find that your spouse is gay, there are different feelings in place. Anytime a marriage ends in divorce, it is not a pleasant situation. Part of the problem is that we love the way we were taught to love. We have this "Prince Charming/Cinderella" mentality. Added to this is sexual intimacy, and when we give of ourselves in this way and that gift is no longer wanted, for whatever the reason, we react, well, **humanly.**

I will offer some perspective from my own perch of hindsight and I hope it helps. Realize that your spouse does love you. You are probably one of the few members of the opposite sex that he or she cares about enough to consider trying to live a heterosexual life with. They may be questioning a lot of their desires and feel that if they immerse themselves in a heterosexual life that any of those desires will go away. They may not have any idea when they begin the relationship that they are gay. It may only be after years of living in a relationship that doesn't just feel quite right that they acknowledge this about themselves. The last thing that you need to come to accept for your own piece of mind is – they do not set out to hurt you.

When we are hurt and offended by anyone, it is our choice. I understand that now. What we often perceive as betrayal is just a person expressing who they are. If we fault them, it is our choice to do so. They are expressing their truths. This is also true in heterosexual relationships. The end of a relationship is painful in any circumstance and for any reason. Keep in mind, however, it is only as painful as we allow it to be. Most of all I would say to everyone, work for gay rights so that anyone is free to love whomever they want. Thirty years ago, a gay man or woman had to enter into a heterosexual relationship if they wanted a family. God doesn't care who we love, only that we **do** love.

I met a special man one time. We knew each other briefly, but significantly, and long enough to share many philosophical conversations. Most of those talks were on the phone, but there were three or four times in a ten year period that we were able to spend a few days together. I was in Los Angeles for training for a business that I was getting into. Ken was there for meetings that had to do with his engineering business. We met one evening when I was with a group of women and he was there with a couple of other guys. We all talked, danced, and had a pleasant evening. He and I ran into each other the next night and we got to talking, as strangers do. We were able to talk about things with each other that we couldn't talk to another soul about. We didn't have any prior relationship with each other, knew none of the same people, and didn't even live in the same country. For all we assumed, we would never see each other again. At that time, I did not yet know that Don was gay, I just knew I was miserable. I thought this three week training would let him realize what life would be like without me, and he would want to mend the marriage. Ken and I talked about relationships in general and both of ours specifically. He said something that has stuck with me over the years since we met, "It is unrealistic and unfair to expect one person to meet 100% of your needs 100% of the time. None of us can do that for any other person yet that is what we expect in our relationships-especially marriage."

Love is all there is, but we don't really understand it. It is pure love of others' spirits (as being one with ours) that will lead to joy in life, not the selfish kind of love that we so often indulge in., We set ourselves up to be disappointed by having unrealistic expectations. When we love, unconditionally, that is exactly what it means-without conditions. A former student and Facebook friend, Shannon, summed it up beautifully. I asked the question, "How do you define love personally?" Her answer, "I can't define it but it feels like sunshine on the inside." That is the entire point of love, it permeates your spirit so much that you are literally light from within.

CHAPTER EIGHTEEN

I don't know how you feel about angels, but I have always believed in them, at least in theory. If you need proof of their existence, you only have to watch *It's a Wonderful Life,* and you will be introduced to Clarence. I have no idea how old I was when I first saw that movie, but every time I watch it I have thought it would be so great to see how I have impacted others' lives. George Bailey had impacted everyone so positively, it just always bring me to tears. He had no idea of his sphere of influence until one night during his encounter with Clarence. I look back at all of the time that I have let opportunities pass by that could have been more positive, and figure that I might not fare as well as George. In the recognizing and accepting of this past, I become thankful for those opportunities because they have led me to here, now. In this awareness, there is the potential for great growth. If you need more proof, there was *Highway to Heaven* and *Touched by an Angel.* Angels exist. God sends us only angels. We are all angels for others. Every person we encounter in life has a gift for us and we have a gift for them because we are angels too.

After sixteen frustrating years of trying to get a transfer from a fifth grade classroom to a third grade assignment, the school corporation decided to move me. They sent me to Clark Middle School to teach sixth grade science! This was not my idea of funny, but there was little I could do if I wanted to remain employed; so, transfer it was. I was trained to work in all areas of education with children. I did not have a focused area of study like junior high and high school teachers are required to have. I was put in a science class because I was one of the few grade school teachers being transferred that did not have a fear of science, I actually enjoyed it.

It was shortly after transferring that I met the principal's wife, Ann, and discovered we had a shared passion for gardening. We quickly became friends. We have been best of friends for about twenty-five years. She is one of the nicest, kindest, most generous-spirited people I have ever met. Kind, gentle, and nice were not three adjectives that would have been used to describe me on any day at any time. I would tell her that going to the middle school was not all bad because I would never have met her if that had not happened. Then I would smile and say, "but...maybe God put me there so that **you** could meet **me!**" People cross our paths at the time they are supposed to for a purpose. There are no coincidences. Ann saw in me things that I didn't see. She knew there was more there than I could accept about myself. I would try to remain crabby and tough but she knew there was someone else within that was trying to find a way out. I love her to pieces, always have, and always will. She is truly one of my most loved angels.

Another angel is my sister, Mary Ann. My younger sister by three-and-a-half years, she has always been a source of irritation to me. She would pester me to the limits of my tolerance but if I pushed her down or hit her, I was the one who would get into trouble-go figure. Like I say, always an irritation. I posted on Facebook that my New Year's Resolution this year was to take "Pollyanna" pills more often than "Maxine" pills. Not too long after that, she had a rough day and she said that she was feeling more like Maxine and she wanted Pollyanna back. That is always what she was, and is, and probably the reason she has irritated me so.

When we were young, she could amuse herself with little effort. She was always happy. She has seemed to enjoy life regardless of what was going on around her, without questions, and without needing to control. I never understood this, nor have I never wanted to have her life, but I have come to realize that the reason she seemed to have a more pleasant life is because she was more pleasant.

It's as simple as that. She was not constantly pushing against what was happening, she was relaxing into the flow of life. We are all on different paths and we each get to our destination which is the realization of who we are. She is retiring this year and I look forward to having an opportunity to spend more time with her. Her ideas and mine are very different. Our approach to life is much different. I am sure we will both learn from each other and hopefully become best of friends.

Everyone who comes into our life is a gift. Everyone is a chance for us to show our God-ness. We decide, whether we realize it or not, to accept this gift graciously or whether we ignore it or reject it. I used to look for a "sign" of what I was supposed to learn. I now look at everything as a sign, a sign whereby I have a chance to give the gifts of kindness, love, and joy. It is in the giving of those gifts that I will receive them back into my life. Anytime we give smiles, words of encouragement, and a freely accepting attitude, we are opening ourselves up to receiving the best life has to offer. We have a chance to let our soul experience the freedom it needs. When our soul is free we can experience joy and happiness from within.

CHAPTER NINETEEN

Do I think of good and evil? Yes, I do, but I am not sure that God does. This is another circular topic with me, because it also encompasses the concepts of heaven and hell.

If God, who is good, and the Devil, who is evil, both exist, then we have to look at our belief that God is all-powerful. If He is all-powerful, why doesn't He just get rid of the Devil and, hence, evil? Perhaps it is because good and evil are just dualities like hot and cold, short and tall. Perhaps it is all relative. Perhaps the Devil was only created as an illustration on that scale to help us understand the differences. Dr. Martin Luther King, Jr., expressed it. "There is some evil in the best of us, and some good in the worst of us." That seems to be a pretty accurate statement.

If God (our source energy-the energy that is present in everyone as the soul) is all-powerful then it doesn't make sense that He couldn't take care of the Devil, if one actually existed. Why would a loving God allow evil to exist, then sit on a throne waiting for some to do evil deeds, then damn us to hell for eternity. This does not make any sense, whatsoever. This is not the way a loving God would behave. What would the all-powerful source of everything have to prove anyway, His power? And, who would He have to prove it to, Himself?

The human creation of a devil character comes about when we consider "free will." Because we choose our actions and they often bring undesired results, we have something, or in this case, someone (the devil) to fall back on, to blame for the problems and the consequences. How often do you hear Christians talking about, "it was the work of the devil." Might it just be more accurate to say, "Well, they certainly made a crappy choice and they will have to live with it and deal with the consequences." Blaming an evil force absolves us of the consequences of our actions. It implies that we had no choice in the matter, it was all the Devil's fault.

After thinking a lot about evil, and what I would consider evil, I decided that evil experiences occur as a result of a choice made by a human that reflects a pandering to ego's needs rather than soul's needs. Once again, thoughts and attitudes come into the mix. Perception of evil is different for everyone.

I've already addressed hell a bit earlier so you know my thoughts on that subject began many years ago. I believe in heaven and hell, but I believe in them differently than I think most people might. I don't believe hell is a place you go after you die. I don't believe hell is a place at all. I can't even believe in death anymore. We are eternal spiritual beings with a physical body, not the other way around. Our spirit or soul lives on this earth for a blink of an eye, or less, in this physical body which is every changing. It is what we create in this time that gives us a chance to experience hell or heaven while we are here. I believe hell to occur when we try to stay separate from God and each other. We will experience that oneness again when our soul is freed from its earthly physical confines and thus we will be in Heaven again. We do not need to wait until our physical body no longer exists I believe we can attain oneness with the Source of all that was, is and ever will be, and experience the joy that we call Heaven here and now.

We are told in the Bible and other words of God that we need to go within to find God, or Heaven. If we give any validity to the research of Gregg Braden, this becomes literal in that our cells are encoded with God's signature. All we need to do is find, from within, that which connects us to our Source and we will have found heaven. If God intended a perfect world, He would have created it to begin with. I guess He did, and we have called it Eden. Now, if He had wanted it to stay perfect, would He have created a serpent to entice Adam and Eve? Again, it doesn't make sense. Another thing to consider is that we are told it was only when Adam and Eve caved in to the apple that is was discovered they had been in paradise all along. Without anything to compare it to, they couldn't have known they were there. If that holds true for Adam and Eve, then perhaps it holds true for us also. We are able to experience Heaven or Eden when we make that choice; but, we are too busy fearing what will happen to us at our physical death to make choices and accept the oneness that is literally within us all already.

CHAPTER TWENTY

Do you think that God really cares if you go to a certain building on a certain day to worship Him? Do you think He cares if we worship Him at all, is that why He created us so that we could pay homage to Him? Do you think He has a vested interest in exactly how or when we talk to Him? Every day is Holy, every minute is Holy, and every place is Holy. We get communications from God every minute. It is when we look around in appreciation for everything that we are communicating back with Him. Every minute can become a communication and communion with God if we choose. Our soul comes into a finite body to experience God by co-creating a joyous, loving, abundant life.

God doesn't have an ego. I can't figure out any reason whatsoever that He would have for making all the rules and rituals that churches of all faiths seem to think that He has. Those rules and rituals have been created by man, not God. I believe He is always here for all of us, every way, every day, regardless of what sacred text we use, regardless of what name we call Him. All of the magnificence of God is love. He does not have the ego needs that we do to prove anything. We limit God so much with our beliefs that give Him human characteristic.

Just as surely as the blood in my arm is the same as the blood in my leg, so it is with our relationship with God. Blood cannot be any different than what it is, regardless of which part of the body it comes from and it is all one. So it is with God and us-we are part of Him and He is part of us. God knows this; therefore, He has no reasons to restrict us. He knows, even if we have forgotten it, that we are all one. He is aware that we are never **not** a part of Him. He exhibits unconditional love for us all. What happens if we profess to have no love for Him? What happens if your own children turn their back on you, leave home, and refuse to talk to you? Does it keep you from looking forward to having them come back home? If we, as physical humans, can do this, do you not think that the Source we are a part of is even more loving and forgiving?

CHAPTER TWENTY-ONE

One day I was sitting at the deli in the casino having lunch. I began noticing how people moved around. The casino has boldly patterned carpet where the machines set. Plain-colored carpet marks the paths from one area to another. That must be what blood cells look like traveling through the arteries and veins in our body. Perhaps, we are like a planet for all of those trillions of cells. Our bodies are the life force for Earth. What if, because the atom has the same configuration as the solar system, our whole Solar System is but one cell in God's body? Our bodies, our planet, even our entire Solar system is indescribably infinitesimal when considered in that sphere. The Universe is infinite – never ending. When I was young I thought about the sky, and space, going on and on. There must be a place where it stops. What would be there? The only answer I could come up with was – more sky. So it is with God-never ending.

Scientists talk about the time-space continuum and I get confused quickly. (Remember I am from Indiana. Most of the state is on the same time as New York City except for the few counties in the southern part of that state that are on the same time as Chicago. Factor in Daylight Savings time and you might as well be speaking a foreign language.) What I do understand is that if we believe Einstein's Theory of Relativity then time and space are simply measurements we use to explain both. They are relative-space being here and there; and, time to explain now and then. They are relative to the space you are discussing at the time. Einstein himself explained it in this way, "When you are courting a nice girl, an hour seems like a second. When you sit on a red hot cinder a second seems like an hour. That's Relativity."

"Now" is all we have. The past is only significant to us when we allow it to help make our future experiences what we want them to be. If we have made mis-steps and constantly beat ourselves up by continuing to dwell on them, we are giving them attention that does not serve our purpose, which is to lead a joyous life. Look at your thoughts now and use those thoughts to draw to you experiences you desire. If I make "now" the best it can be for me and others then my "past" will be filled with wonderful memories and my "future" is filled with the best it can become. I look into the future knowing that my desires will come to me on time and however they will come. It has become an exciting prospect indeed.

Living in the "now" eliminates doubt and worry. It allows me to look at a rainy day with as much gratitude as I do a sunny day. A dip in the temperatures reminds me that, "this to, shall pass." Before we know it, there will be summer days filled with all the warmth we want, maybe on some days more than we want, which leads us to remembering the cold days, knowing they will come back to us. All of life is cyclical. The coldness of winter gives way to the birth of blooms in spring. This leads to summer and the falling of blooms so the fruit can develop. In the autumn of the year the fruits ripen and we are led back to that time of rest we call winter. We cannot rush the ripening of the tomatoes, the booms of the purple coneflower or the birthing of a baby. It all takes the time it needs to fulfill the promise of its intent.

There is a site on Facebook that had posted a video of physicists discussing what they simply called "possibility." In this documentary the discussion of the theory of quantum physics considered the fact that what we perceive as reality is actually possibility. What we think is reality is not, in that none of it is ultimate reality. All of it is the possibility of consciousness, whether it be a collective consciousness by people worldwide to change the future of the planet or by an individual who can create their own reality by the power of that which they truly perceive to be real. If we work through this thought knowing that energy exploded to create things and that we are co-creator by being part of that creation then we could indeed, through our concentrated thought, create our reality, good or bad, into being.

For instance, if we believe we are going to be sick, then the reality of that shows up in our lives. We don't do this consciously; after all, no one wants to be sick, but if we determine that it is what will happen, then it usually does. People rush to get flu shots because they think they will get the flu. After they get the shot, they will tell you they got it because they were worried they might get the flu and obviously they are still concentrating on those thoughts. Experience and statistics show us that even with the shots a great many people still get the flu. Every cold we catch only adds to our belief that colds and germs are something over which we have no control. Taking care of our bodies by following a good diet, rich in vitamins and minerals with foods that we know to be healthy, breathing in some fresh air, maybe some exercise, maybe these positive activities pursued with the idea, "I am healthy," would be a better route. I recall many time when I was teaching and raising two young children that I literally didn't think about the flu because I didn't have time to get sick. I was too busy to be sick, to think about being sick, and to even have it enter my mind and it didn't happen.

The same documentary stated that we have an incredible number of thoughts (up to seventy thousand per day) only a fraction of which we are aware. This being the case, if we become observers of what flows through our minds, we can choose to accept or dismiss any of those thoughts we wish. When we concentrate on the thoughts that encourage our view of our future and hold to those, we are then becoming co-creators of the reality we choose.

There was also some photographic documentation of a study that I had only previously read about. I have since seen it on Facebook several times. This is the result of years of research by Dr. Masaru Emoto. The research has to do with the crystalline structure of a molecule of water. If, on a jar of water, the words are written: "thanks," "I love you," and "joy", the water develops a beautiful crystalline structure that looks very much like an elaborate three dimensional snowflake. On the other hand if, on a jar of water, the words, "fear," "I hate you" and "anger" are written, the crystalline structure will be deformed looking. The photograph of this structure actually looked like a picture you see in a health magazine of viruses and diseases. It was a greenish, cloudy, blobby lump. In this case, one picture was truly worth a thousand words. Because our bodies are about seventy-five percent water, the message seems crystal clear (pun intended). Our entire bodies will react much differently physiologically to good messages of a positive, kind nature than they will to self-defeating negative messages. The difference we will feel will have to be radiated from us to others, I can think of no other way that we would react.

CHAPTER TWENTY-TWO

Our thoughts, our attention to those thoughts, and our belief that we control our ability to direct our destinies can make a world of difference in how we perceive our reality. Once we begin to accept the idea that we can become that which we desire, it cannot help but make a difference in the world around us. Think of all the people you interact with on any given day. Who they are is reflected in their outward expression of themselves. A friend recently said to me that you could think you knew a person but until you saw their posts on Facebook, you didn't really know them. I knew what she meant. That which we share with others is a reflection of who we are, or more importantly, who we feel we are. What comes from within is the most important thing that we can experience. If, deep within us, we allow hate and prejudice to fester, that is how we will appear to others and that is what shows up in our reality. It can be no other way. If we allow love, kindness and gratitude to come from within, then that is what others see in us and that will be what shows up in our reality.

I believe people are often so mired in feelings of self-doubt and lack that they believe this is the reality to which they are doomed. I say that because for most of my life, I would have believed that everything in this book would have been too unrealistic for me to apply to my life. I am telling you that you are not doomed, you can make shifts in your thoughts and attitudes – bits at a time- that will make miraculous changes in your life. Look around and observe. Find **one** thing that can put a smile on your face. We all have something that makes us smile, even briefly. Concentrate on that smile, that thought, that observation, and the feeling you get from that observation or memory; find something, anything, for which you can be thankful. Concentrate on the feeling of gratitude and hold that feeling as long as you can. Revisit these two thoughts and feelings as often as you can. Observe more often and feel more often. The more you practice this, the more often you will find things that make you smile and things for which to be grateful. This is how you start. Your hard edges will soften and your life will begin to change. It is not an overnight process, there just needs to be a desire to change on your part and as you can look around, wherever you are in life right now, and find things to be thankful for and things to feel joyous about, more opportunities for those things will be attracted to you. You will begin to see your kinship with oneness, with all of life. You will be back on your path to a more fulfilled life. As Dr. Dyer would say, "Change the way you look at things and the things you look at will change."

Albert Einstein is quoted as saying, "Look deep into nature, then you will understand everything better." An appreciation of nature cannot be over-emphasized. We are a part of nature and when we immerse ourselves in it we gain a closer connection to our Source and our soul sings with pleasure. Think of an acorn dropping on the ground, being buried by a squirrel and beginning to grow the next spring. Look at a huge standing oak tree and the magnificence of it. Consider how many gale winds it has withstood and how it is still standing, giving off oxygen for us to breathe and providing us with shade and a home for other inhabitants of the Earth. All of life is so interconnected and we are a part of it. Watch a spider spin her web. It is a fantastic, awe-inspiring process and consider that every species of spider spins their webs differently and for various purposes. Think of wild blackberries growing freely, providing food for the birds, and, if we are fortunate, for us. Einstein also told us, "Our task must be to free ourselves by widening our circle of compassion to embrace all living creatures and the whole of nature and its beauty." It is when we accept ourselves as one with all the magnificence on the planet, that we can vibrationally feel our own magnificence and radiate the love, joy, and appreciation that we feel from deep within.

Playing, running unencumbered, swinging, and imagining life to be anything we wanted it to be, that is how we lived life as a child. There are three quotes-again from Albert Einstein-that serve to show the importance of our imagination:

1. Imagination is everything. It is the preview of life's attractions
2. Logic will get you from A to B. Imagination will take you everywhere.
3. Imagination is more important than knowledge.

One of our greatest gifts is that of imagination. Anything we can imagine, we can create into our reality. Children are not fearful and critical, they use their imagination freely and express joy spontaneously. We need to emulate them and not teach them to mimic us. When we have a desire, we can use our imagination to help give us the feeling we would have if we already have our desire. We can use this feeling to raise ourselves vibrationally so that what we desire will flow to us. The subconscious mind does not know if the feeling is based on something real or something imagined, it only acts on the feeling of having it already. Use your imagination to help draw your desires to you. You cannot just imagine having something and have it come to you. You have to believe and feel that it is already yours. Believe before you see it, know that when you ask, it is given, and feel the feeling of already having it. Relax and know that when the time and circumstances are right, it will be yours.

Because of the Law of Attraction, the longer we think about something, the more attention we give to it, and the more frequently we return to that thought, the stronger the vibrational alignment becomes. Every thought we have, when we give it our attention, expands and becomes part of our vibration and is invited into our experience. This occurs whether it is something we want or something we don't want. The Law of Attraction is about inclusion only. It excludes nothing. By that, I mean if we have a thought about something we don't want and we focus on it, and keep saying, for example, "I don't want to be sick," "I hope I don't get sick," saying "no" to it, doesn't help. The very fact that you are focusing on it at all includes it in your experience. You need to keep only the thoughts, "I am healthy" in your mind to have the flow of health coming to you. You must align yourself vibrationally only to the things you wish to show up in your life. Once we accept that, we then start wondering how we will know if we are getting that vibrational alignment. Our emotions will give us our answer. Your feelings mirror your vibrations.

When we ask for something, knowing that it will be given, without exception, we then have to tune our vibrations in a way that will allow us to accept it. The way you feel indicates your allowing or resisting what you desire. In *Ask and It is Given*, Abraham tells, "It is not possible for you to consistently feel positive emotion about something and have it turn out badly, just as it is not possible for you to consistently feel bad about something and have it turn out well-for the way you feel will tell you if you are allowing your natural Well-Being or not." (665 of 2970 -22% - Kindle edition)

By directing your thoughts to more positive thoughts that create better emotions, you gain the vibrational alignment you need to attract that which you are seeking. Any time you are appreciating something you are a vibrational match to who you are and the better you feel. If you are finding fault with a situation or another person, you are offering a vibration that has a lower frequency and you will be offering resistance to that which you want to attract. As you become more aware of your thoughts and accept only those highest thoughts you will get the best feelings. This will help you achieve a closer connection to your source and you become co-creator of the reality you wish to see.

You cannot let yourself dwell on how or when your desire comes to you. The laws of the universe are already working. If you dwell on the fact that it is not already here, the subconscious will see your focus on the "not having" as a different directive and work toward giving you the "not having." Whatever you give focused thought to becomes activated so you need to keep your thoughts focused positively on what you desire. Imagine how you will feel when it comes to you. When you keep your thoughts focused in this way, you don't want to think of anything other than the realization of your desire and how you will feel when it gets here. Have no doubts, know that it is on its way. Abraham once again tells us, "Anything that you give your attention to will become your "truth," The Laws of Attraction says that it must. Your life and everyone else's too, is but a reflection of the predominance of your thoughts. There is no exception to this." (*Ask and It is Given*, 7171 of 2970 – 23% - Kindle edition.)

CHAPTER TWENTY-THREE

I sat watching squirrels one day and continually ran through my mind just one thing, "Am I just losing it?" What if all of this reading is just philosophical mumbo-jumbo, or, like Andrew says, "Woo-woo." Can it really be that there is truly a Law of Attraction that can help everyone have a life they want to have? Then I remembered my life, my thoughts, and my feelings a year before and I knew that what I was reading and absorbing represented truth for me or it would not have affected my life so profoundly. I felt as though I were reconnecting with something that had been there, but lost for a very long time. I was seeing the world with new eyes and I realized I was now viewing life through the eyes of my soul. I am experiencing Heaven. My doubts were created by an ego that would like to see me remain fearful. If I suspend the ego and not be continually discontented with my life, is that not a good thing? I determined that I am on the path that is that of oneness with my source and that path is where I am choosing to stay so that I can continue to express joy, love, peace, and harmony while I am here. I have found my truth. We are all one with God, we are all one with each other and all living beings; We are not separate, what hurts me hurts you, what hurts you hurts me and all there is – is love. I am experiencing life at a level I had not known existed. I am looking forward to every day with anticipation of what will unfold. I am no longer judging family and friends, I am finding less and less reasons to criticize, and I have little need to control anyone or any situation. I am accepting life, knowing that there may be ups and downs before my desires come to me, but I know that what I desire will come to me in its own time. Worry and doubt seldom find their way into my thoughts, and when they do, I am able to dismiss them and not dwell on them. I am experiencing happiness by allowing myself to **be** happy.

Some of the reading that I have done suggests meditation. It is a way in which we can slow down all of our thoughts by concentrating on silence and stillness. It allows us to be calm and accepting of life. When we do this, we get the opportunity to help transcend negative thoughts and emotions. When I hear the term, "meditation," I picture sitting on a rice mat in a Yoga-like Lotus position humming and chanting my way to harmony. I see it a bit differently now. Anytime we are able to slow our thoughts and experience calm and silence, we are in a meditative state. I have realized that the time I spend in silence of night gazing at the moon and stars is my best meditation. I let the immensity surround me and feel that I am part of all creation. It is extremely relaxing and satisfying because I seem to drift into that oneness state quite easily anymore. When I kept thinking I had to meditate in just a certain way, I remained frustrated. If you have ever been sitting with a cat on your lap and just felt the softness of the fur as you petted her over and over, you have meditated. If you have watched the sunset disappear beyond the horizon in quiet solitude, you have meditated. Another place I can freely let myself drift into that quiet contemplative state is in the shower. There I can feel the tension and worries go right down the drain and enjoy the experience of letting go of everything and relaxing into nothing all at the same time.

I have found that any situation has become better when I look at the nature around me and acknowledge the abundance I have. There are about 8.7 million species of life on our planet and somewhere between 86% on land and 91%marine that have yet to be named and classified. That verifies an abundant planet. When we perceive lack and concentrate on lack; that is what will come to us in our experience. When there are bills to pay and not enough money in the checking account to cover them, we are experiencing a temporary lack; that is true. It is not that abundance cannot exist for us, it already does, we have not been allowing it in because of our negative thoughts concerning it, and because we are concentrating on our appearance of lack. If we determine that abundance exists and we will find a better way to experience that abundance, and concentrate on the abundance flowing into our experience, then we will be presented with opportunities of that kind. As long as you are anticipating the abundance that is coming your way, things will begin to change in your experience. If we determine that we will find a better way to tap into abundance, the intent to get into that abundant flow will present opportunities. Maybe another job, part-time, is all that is needed. If so, that opportunity will present itself. The Law of Attraction will attract to us what is needed to supply our desire.

Also evident when we talk about abundance is to get a clear understanding of it. When we think of only extra money in our pockets we overlook the flow of abundance. When we use coupons to get money off of an object we purchase, we experience the flow of abundance. It has been suggested keeping a record for a week of all examples of that flow in our lives. I caught myself overlooking things like picking up a penny or being invited out for dinner. They both represent the flow, but I was still limiting my concept. When we change the way we look at things we truly open our eyes to all of the opportunities that can change our experiences. I am able to accept all the abundance coming to me and through me and be very thankful that I am getting to experience this flow.

Thankfulness, gratitude, and appreciation cannot be stressed enough either. If we do not appreciate what we have, then we will probably not be appreciative of more. Most of us are taught from an early age to be glad for what we have because there are many people in the world who are living with much less. I am extremely thankful that I am writing this book because I know that everyone who reads it will take **something** from it that will help them live their life more fully, more generously and more lovingly. As I write it, those feelings are more pronounced in me. They will be more appreciative and grateful for the world around us and all the opportunities we have to experience lift to its fullest. I readily admit that I had interest in monetary gain when I first heard about manifesting. I have been very fortunate in life and I have always known this on one level; but, I must say that I took most of my blessings for granted. If I was having a difficult time financially, an opportunity presented itself for a part-time job or business opportunity that I heartily embraced. At one time while I was raising the kids, I was teaching, running a retail business, and had an herbal crafting and gardening business on the side. Abundance was flowing through my life, but I was only seeing what I perceived as lack.

When we think of money and abundance as the same thing, we miss out on a very important concept. Money is simply something we use to exchange for something else. It is paper, that's all, paper that has an assumed value to someone else. Abundance is something greater. It includes money, but it also includes the total abundant life experiences. I think these abundant experiences are the kind of "riches" that the Bible is referring to when we are told the riches of the Kingdom will be ours.

There once was a man back-packing on a trip through a beautiful land. As he was walking along, he noticed there were gold nuggets of all sizes on the ground. He picked them up, grateful for his good fortune. He picked up enough that they began to get very heavy but he still held on to then, knowing they would finance his journey. He came into a town and found a place to stay for the night. Upon checking in, he placed on of the gold nuggets on the counter, knowing it would be more than enough to pay for his evening's lodging. The clerk looked at the nugget, than at the man, and asked, "Why are you giving me this worthless rock? I am going to need sand to pay for the room." The gold only held value to the one who perceived it as having value. To someone else it was worthless. So too, it is with us. Paper money only has us in its grip because that is where we are placing our value. When we have an abundant life, then money no longer has that hold on us. There are some people whose life is so rich, so completely abundant with friends and family that if the monetary system were to collapse tomorrow and they were literally penniless, it would not matter. It is my goal to have that kind of abundant life to appreciate as I traverse this path called life.

CHAPTER TWENTY-FOUR

It is when we accept and know that abundance will flow through us, that our needs will be met; then we begin to distinguish between needs and wants. Mahatma Gandhi is paraphrased with the following quote, "Earth provides enough to satisfy every man's needs, but not every man's greed." Needs around the world are not being met, obviously, when 30,000 children a day die of starvation. It is not because the abundance is not there, it is because of the greed of some that needs are not met. What is done to one is done to all of us. I cannot help everyone in the world, none of us can. But, each and every one of us can help someone. It reminds me of a story I have always found inspiring: One morning at the beach a man was walking along after a night of storms. He came upon a young boy who was picking up starfish, one by one, from the hundreds that had been washed ashore, and throwing them back into the ocean. The man asked the boy what he was doing and the boy told him that he was saving the starfish. He then told the boy," You can't make a difference, you know, you can't save them all." The little boy picked another one up, tossed into the ocean, looked at the man and said, "I saved that one." That is how abundance works. We give what we can, when we can, and to whomever we can. We share. Share the abundance, let it flow through you to everyone you come in contact with in some way.

Awareness can give us the impetus to make changes either individually or globally. When we think life is strumming along and we are relegated to whatever fate has in store for us, we feel we are powerless. Life is a result of what we think and who we decide we want to be. We have what we have because of who we are and how closely we are aligned with our source. Look at some of our most revered Masters and Teachers. None of them espoused worldly trappings. They were content with who they were and knew that all needs were met. Needs can be reduced to air, food, water, and shelter. The UN puts out a Development Report. It consists of three parts: Inequality-adjuster, Gender Inequality Index, and the Multidimensional Poverty Index (MPI). I became aware of this publication in some of the research I was doing. Figures given from the nineteen nineties indicated that the money spent on cosmetics and ice cream could have provided basic education and basic sanitation worldwide. The amount spent on pet food would have funded basic health and nutrition needs worldwide. We are all "missing the mark" to allow this to continue. Abundance exists but it is in the unequal distribution and use of this abundance that we perceive lack. As more people become aware of their individual responsibility, a shift in the consciousness of the whole will reflect a change. Right now, collectively, these conditions are deemed "okay" or it would change. When enough people see a necessity to change their world, experiences in the world will change. When we truly embrace abundance and combine it with the realization that we are all one, we will not want to see others going without basic necessities of life. We will want to see their lives be joyous, as all are intended to live. We will want this for others as much as we want it for ourselves.

When we look historically at the mass murders of the American Indian and the Jewish Holocaust, we cannot help but see this is true. These atrocities, and ones being committed today in time of war, were the results of an entire world who did not stand up and say that this was not how we wanted humanity to express itself. Does not everyone have a right to be able to exist without fear from another group? It was not until the conscious of the multitudes said "no more" did things change. Keep in mind, however, it is the individual consciousness that makes up the collective consciousness. Just like the little boy with the starfish, we need to do our part. When we are attuned to our Source, we see the need for personal responsibility. That responsibility is easy to ascertain when we know that we are all one. Whatever deed is done to anyone is also done to us. We are all one, indivisible. God cannot be divided and neither can we. It is in knowing and being aware of our oneness that we can become who we really are. We can enter each day with a sense of kindness and gratitude. We look around and want to see everyone share in the abundance of all. Anthropologist Margaret Mead, once said: "Never doubt that a small group of thoughtful, committed citizens can change the world; indeed, it's the only thing that ever has."

CHAPTER TWENTY-FIVE

I have always had a quick smile and have been able to see humor easily in most situations. It has had a way of getting out even during my most troubling times. It has been one aspect of my personality that has, in some ways, been my salvation. When we are able to see lightness and hopefulness in our darkest times, we can be thankful. Even thought I could smile and laugh, rarely did I feel it down to my heart. It penetrated me at times, like the days both of my children were born. For the most part it did not permeate me. The smile I carry now is one of complete acceptance of my life and my blessings and I smile even more deeply. It is joy beyond belief, happiness that cannot accurately be described. I have been thinking lately that perhaps this is what is referred to as "bliss." It certainly seems like it. At times, I think I may look rather goofy going around with this smile on my face for no apparent reason, but I just can't help it.

I am no longer concerned about what will happen to me tomorrow. I am choosing my life with conscious awareness. I know now that thoughts can be tossed aside or incorporated into who I am and who I choose to be. I allow negative thoughts to pass on by on that conveyor belt of life and dwell only on those thoughts that give me the highest vibration. Only the thoughts of love, happiness, joy, kindness, and gratitude are taken off that conveyor belt. Any thoughts we dwell on are included in what we attract. It takes concentrated effort if you have a lot of negativity, but the rewards outweigh the effort.

There are only two emotions that all others spring from. One of those is fear. When we fear life, we are consumed with worry, doubt, pessimism and anger. Most of how we react when we are coming from fear is negatively expressed. We judge others, we criticize and condemn. We use our love as surely as we would a weapon. We give it when others are only doing things that we approve of and withhold it when they are not. We give only to those people we feel are worthy. We scorn the person in front of us at the grocery check-out when they pull out their food stamp card. We condemn those who don't have jobs. We live in a state of discontent that we don't have enough and won't be good enough. We are stingy with others and express little thanks for what we do have. We fear life, we fear death, we fear hell, and worst of all, we fear God. We see him as a vengeful being just waiting for us to mess up so he can shake his scepter and lock the Pearly Gates.

The other emotion is love. When we love life, how things change. We are thankful every day. We look for ways we can express our love for life and others by acts of kindness and generosity. We look for ways to serve others. We make conscious decisions not to judge, criticize or condemn because we do not know what is happening to that other person and what path their life is taking. We are thankful that others are able to get food for their family. We are optimistic about the days ahead. We know that life is for living, death does not end anything but our brief temporary existence on the physical plane. We express ourselves freely to others. We react with kindness and grace to all of those we encounter. If there is a way that we can extend a helping hand, we try to do so. We do what we can, when we can, in whatever way we can for whomever needs our help. We no longer allow worry, doubt, and anger to cloud our days.

I have always been dependent on others and outside circumstances to make me happy. If I had money in my purse, I was happy. If someone loved me-the way I thought they should love me, I was happy. If I got to take a vacation, I was happy. It was a brief time of being happy that ended as soon as the episode was over, if it even lasted that long. I collected "things" – happy when I could purchase yet another village house or collectible basket. After the purchase was made, I went back to looking for something else to collect. There was no stopping. I looked at all the stuff and didn't know why I wasn't happy. I certainly should have been, I thought. I wanted something and found a way to get it. That should have been enough. I took the same approach with fabric when I began quilting. I stopped at every quilt shop I found and bought fabric. I did not see that I was trying to fill something that was never going to be filled with "things" no matter how much I accumulated.

Now I had a houseful of stuff and nowhere to put it all. I made a conscious effort about fifteen years ago to simplify my life and began getting rid of some of the stuff that, at one time, had been so very important for me to acquire. When I moved to Anderson I got rid of a great deal more and have donated much since the move. It is my goal to continue that. I see now that my needs are more than taken care of and to have more than that has now become excess that I want to slough off. Those purchases were made in attempt to prove something to myself, to prove my worth, to fill up the void that was created by my feelings of inadequacy and unworthiness. My wardrobe is simple but I still have clothes I don't wear. What is it about me and shower gel? I counted thirteen unopened bottles of shower gel. Obviously, when we buy like that we are thinking of lack rather than abundance. When we live in fear we see lack. When we feel lack that is what we will experience. When we are thankful for what we have, knowing that we have all we need, that blessings flow to us.

God, Source, Holy Spirit, Eternal Mother, Allah, Jehovah, whatever we choose to call it, is everywhere. There is no place it is not. It is in nature, it is our nature, and it is in each cell. It is the I AM THAT I AM. That Source is with us always and is always communicating with us. Whether we realize that is something else. Our thoughts and feelings are the best forms of communications. It is up to us to determine how God is speaking to us. Our highest thoughts of peace, kindness, and joy are the ones from God. When we continually ignore God's communications we find our lives to be unsatisfying. We are given free will, therefore, we decide what messages we will be open to and what messages we will choose to ignore. We have been sent many messages and messengers. We use a scripture like the Bible and presume that is the only valid message from God. I don't think that God has any one chosen group of people that He views as special. Is it important that we confine ourselves to a set of rules and live in constant fear that we are interpreting these rules correctly? If you believe that your religious book is your guide and your only guide, then that is your path. I am finding that for me, the Bible is having additional spiritual guidance added to it. I do not accept it as my only message. I believe that God is greater than any of us can imagine.

I find Buddhist teachings of great value. Buddhists recognize that all people need to have a religious system that enhances their path and they respect all religious beliefs even though they do not believe in the same doctrines. "All major religious traditions carry basically the same message: that is love, compassion, and forgiveness. The important thing is they should be part of our daily lives."(His Holiness the XIV Dalai Lama) He also states, "My religion is very simple. My religion is kindness." He not only follows the teaching of Buddha, but also reflects those altruistic teachings to all with whom he interacts.

CHAPTER TWENTY-SIX

Much information is based in the physics of how the Universe works. Since my son is a physicist, I turned to him for some explanations and clarifications. Much of what he says I admit I don't understand. What I do understand is that all of what we experience is basically energy vibrations. Fastest vibrations are attracted to fastest vibrations (like attracts like) **but** within the vibration, it is the proton (with a positive charge) and the electron (with a negative charge) that are attracted for matter to form. There is also some thought that what we see is what we expect to see. What we perceive as a solid has more space **between** the atoms than it has atoms itself, yet we perceive a solid. Just as we pass through the gas around us (air) it is conceivable that creatures with a great deal more mass than we have could be (theoretically) passing in and around us in much the same way that we pass through the air around us. When we say that all is relative, it takes on a more significant meaning. What it means is that our sensory perceptions may be, to some extent, illusions.

Religion can't explain science and science can't explain religion. If my beliefs were based on scientific fact, I couldn't prove the existence of God – I can only feel God. Many scientists and philosophers are coming closer and closer to achieving areas in which both fields can agree, and I find this promising. I use the field of biology and the diversity of nature to prove my belief in the existence of God. My belief, my faith in my truth, is no more valid than yours is, nor is it any less valid. It is only when either of us sets out to prove that "my way is the right way" that we would begin to have problems. When we can truly accept another's belief as "okay" and not try to change them to our way of thinking that we can begin to experience oneness with each other.

When Carolyn, Glenda, Sandy, and I met in Biloxi we had a great time. I think I could spend the rest of my life on the beaches of Biloxi. It is just beautiful. I came home and the three books Sandy had promised to loan me were waiting in the mail: *Conversations with God – Book one*, *Conversations with God – Book three*, and *Communion with God*. While I was reading these books, I noticed that these conversations had begun in 1992. Why, about twenty years later, was I just now hearing of them and reading them so seriously? They are based on a disgruntled writer who wrote a scathing letter to God asking for some answers to questions he had. He then got an answer in the form of a conversation which he refers to as transcribing what God said. Do I believe this was God talking to him? Even if it is not word for word exact, it seems to be inspired by God and that is the same thing. After all, we talk **to** God when we pray, why wouldn't God actually talk **back** to us as well? There is a great deal of wisdom in these books and if God is communicating with us at all times, then, why not? For someone who once told a friend, "God would probably have to slam me in the head with a 2x4 for me to get a message," this was a much less painful method. I found that God was talking to me through these books. Many questions I had been mulling over in my mind for the previous few months became much clearer. One of the interesting things that I got from these books is that God wants us to be happy, all the time. He does not want us to fear him. I find that I am constantly going back to these books and re-reading them, getting more insight into my relationship with God as the source of "All there is."

There was an empty lot at an intersection here in Anderson that I pass three or four times a week. It is a busy intersection with a stop light. Rarely do I not have to stop at the red light. A few weeks ago, I was stopped there again and as I was sitting there, I looked to my left and saw a completed building, a restaurant, already opened with a parking lot full of cars. Now that building did not go from empty lot to fully established business in one or two days. How was it that I had not noticed it was even being built? I think that is what much of our life is that. Truth is all around. Books are written, songs are sung, but all of a sudden we become aware of them. Awareness, the recurring theme in all of the books, and now an example from life. By conscious awareness of our thoughts, we can begin to focus on those that speak to our highest self. When we do that, we become co-creator of our reality.

Emerson, Thoreau, Shakespeare, Einstein, Jung, many writers, artists, psychologists, and philosophers have repeated these truths over and over in many ways but we have still trudged alone unaware. When we wake up and become aware, we can then make a conscious decision about the avenues of life we explore. We are no longer like a ship tossed about on the ocean but we can firmly set sail for the port where we want to seek harbor.

There was a time in my life, that I felt the following to be a perfectly wonderful analogy for my life, and I will share that with you:

I was traveling along on this journey we call life and saw a street that went off into a subdivision. There was a beautifully landscaped entry and it appeared to be full of beautiful homes. I decided to turn in and see the sites. Shortly after I made the turn I saw a "Dead End" sign. I did not totally ignore it. I saw it then decided that maybe it just hadn't been taken down. Even if it did dead end, it wouldn't take much time out of my trip to enjoy what it held. I kept going down the street, the sights were great and I was loving the experience. I then saw another "Dead End' sign; but, what the heck, I was really enjoying this, as much as I had any part of the journey, so I decided it would be worth it, even when I had to turn around. Turn around, I did, six years later!! As I was going back to the main thoroughfare, I could not be sorry that I had taken that street, dead end and all. I was sorry that those sites were finished, but I would have the memories of them when I wanted to recall then. I have decided to regret nothing in life that has given me pleasure and made me smile.

Now I know that both the detours and the beautiful sights are to be treasured. One never knows where the detours will take them or what will be seen along the way. As long as you stay on the road, you will be fine. That road ends up at your destination.

All of life is about the choices we make and where those choices lead. If we find the detours, keep in mind that it is the entire journey that is meant to be beautiful. Conscious awareness occurs when we become the observer of the choices we make and of the effect of our choices. When we live life in this way, we no longer view ourselves as a victim of a haphazard fate.

CHAPTER TWENTY-SEVEN

Just as most of us have a main "scripture" and our own word for "God," we usually have an idea of "heaven." We will all reach heaven, but we can experience heaven right here and right now if we open our eyes to the beauty around us. If we accept heaven into our "now" of physical existence, we open our world to encompass all those we meet. We also embrace all our experiences as part of our physical journey. To do this, we willingly accept the idea of God as Love. Most of the major religions teach this, but even the religions will teach love as a concept that we are to extend to others freely, yet put restrictions on the unconditional love of God for us.

The intricate threads of each of our lives are interwoven to be the tapestry we become. Each tiny individualization serves as but a thread in that tapestry we call humanity. As I review my experiences with an objective eye, I can see and understand that all was the result of how I was feeling or thinking at the time. Because these thoughts of mine were what they were, I drew into my life these experiences.

I believe that God knows all and sees all. If I start thinking a bit deeper, I wonder if he knows the situations we will have presented to us and does He know what we will decide then, because of that decision, will He know what additional situations we will get and what we will decide then? I am not sure anymore that God monitors us quite like that. I am not sure He monitors us at all. He is experiencing His magnificence through us. God is going to welcome us all back when our life on the physical plane, in this physical body, is over. We are not just our bodies, we are spirit and energy in a physical body. This being the case, the free will that God has given us is just that, free to be a Methodist, free to be a Muslim, free to be an Atheist. There are teachers out there for all of us. We are free to hear or we are free to ignore. It doesn't matter to God, because the only thing that He wants is for us to be happy and enjoy our time in this physical incarnation. The soul will be taken care of when it leaves this physical body. It will return from whence it came. It is the spirit of God and God cannot be divided at any time. We are already a part of that Source.

Whatever we do, good or bad, is a cause. What results is the effect. Whatever we cause will have an effect. It is as simple as that in life. If we are doing positive, kind, generous, loving thoughts and acts, those good causes create good effects. If our thoughts and actions are those that reflect jealousy, anger, and ill-will, then the effects reflected will be negative.

It is easy to say, "Be kind," to someone. If that person is not in a place where they can exhibit kindness, not only will your urging not have the desired result, they may go far as to react very negatively. How people react to you is a mirror of how they are feeling. There have been many times when being kind was the last thing I had in mind. I didn't want to be kind, I didn't want to be generous, or loving, or thankful. All I wanted was to be left alone so I could be angry. That happens to many people sometimes. We need to accept those days, we need to accept ourselves just the way we are on any given day in any given circumstance. There is no "right" way or "wrong" way to act and react. When we are able to accept ourselves, noticing the warts, we begin to awaken to our true selves and we can accept others more readily in all circumstances. We can remember that, "This too, shall pass." It is okay. We are all okay, all the time!

If we are sending our "good vibes," we are in that state that slows us to receive that for which we have asked. If we send off bad vibes we are not allowing things to be attracted to us, at least not what we desire. Something will be coming our way, we just won't know what, certainly not our desire. When we emotionally stay in states of anger, depression, and despair, we send off bad vibes and we do not feel good. If we want to live a joyous fulfilled life, we need to get in a place where we can feel the best emotions we are capable of feeling. This may often require direct concentrated effort on our part. Some of us have had years of living in negativity; slipping back into negative thinking and reacting occurs. Every experience we have allows us the opportunity to react to it with our feelings and emotions. When we consciously view these events and circumstances with the very best positive emotions rather than a negative emotion, we are well on our way to leading a more fulfilling life.

CHAPTER TWENTY-EIGHT

When we open ourselves up to learning from any teachings of any religion to help us not only find our path, but also be a light to others, it is then that our path seems much smoother. Jesus was a Master Teacher. Mankind has had many teachers we can learn from. This does not detract from my life as a Christian, but serves to enhance my experience in that it encourages love, which is the example Jesus showed the world when he was here. We are still having teachers placed in our lives. We are all teachers. If our soul is seeking its highest feeling, that of love, when we show love to everyone we encounter, then in that instant we are teachers. God is truth and God is love. God cannot be divided. If we believe these teachings, then anything which comes from fear does not come from God. When our beliefs require us to separate ourselves from others by insisting that our path is the only correct path, we limit God. We place man's restrictions on Him by saying that my scripture is right, yours is wrong, "This path is the right one, you will burn in hell if you don't believe as I do." God doesn't think that way. He is love, no way is he going to choose favorite children and condemn everyone else to eternal punishment. He is bigger than that. Those are man's limitations, not God's. God is not going to create hell so He can keep us in fear that we will end up there. Why would He? What does He have to prove to anyone? He is God. Any belief that induces fear is not from God, who is total love.

Feelings are expressions of the soul. All energy is vibration. If it is the soul's desire to be free and express love, then the feelings of love, joy, and peace are those that would vibrate fastest or more frequently. When we feel the emotions in the higher vibrations, we are experiencing the expansion of the soul and aligning ourselves with the God of our understanding.

CHAPTER TWENTY-NINE

What is sin? That is rather like asking, "What is a weed?" It all depends on who you ask. If you asked Emerson, "What is a weed," the answer would have been, "A plant whose virtues have never been discovered." I will admit to having a pretty loose definition of sin. Perhaps, I have a loose definition of a weed because I personally think that the dandelion is one of the greatest of plants. I have even given talks about the benefits of the dandelion. I don't believe Emerson would have considered it a weed either. It is extremely healthy when cooked like spinach. It benefits bees in the spring before other nectar plants are available to them. The root can be dried and used as a coffee substitute. Canadian researchers are currently looking at the root as a possible cancer cure. What other flower can your children or grandchildren pick to their heart's content and use to present you with a bouquet? Not to mention the fun of blowing the seeds to the wind...Ahhh...such a wonderful plant. Now, you ask most people, and it is the bane of their existence. They don't like the pretty little dandelion at all. They use all sorts of chemicals to get rid of it, dig it out, and mow it down. They just don't want to see it at all.

Sin is simply defined as "missing the mark," In other words, not being the best version of whom we really are. So... is sin the rude way you speak to a clerk or is it playing a card game? Is it dancing, or is it not sharing your sandwich with a friend? Is it smoking, or is it belittling your child for getting a low grade on a spelling test? Some of these actions cause us to miss the mark of what the soul needs to expand and show love for others. We each have to decide which behaviors we consider to be a sin. Some people view dancing as a sin. I have a friend who does not come to the class reunions because they are held where liquor is served. What I would or would not view as sin is unimportant, just as what I would choose is not for anyone else to judge. God doesn't judge our choices. The evolutions of my soul and aligning myself with my Source is my only concern. When I am faced with a choice of any kind, I do as one source suggested. I ask myself, "What would love do?" When I base a decision on the answer to that question, I know that whatever I decided is not missing the mark.

If I had this idea about writing a book and I had done nothing, it would not have been written. I intended to write the book. I intended to get it published. When we intend for something to happen, there is a move in the direction of our intent. When there is an intent to make a change we can remember the words of Ralph Waldo Emerson here also, "Once you make a decision, the Universe conspires to make it happen." If there is no intent in our approach to what we desire, it only amounts to daydreaming. Intent is defined as "an aim or purpose which is accompanied by determination to produce a desired result." According to Dr. Wayne Dyer in his book, _The Power of Intention,_ the definition is expanded to mean not only this but it is also a force in the field of energy in the universe.

This field of energy is everywhere there is no place it does not exist. If you cut open a seed, you do not see the plant, but you know the possibility of it is there. It is the intention of an acorn to become an oak tree, not a tomato plant. It is in this field of intent that we develop as we do. When your ego moves out of the way, you move into this field of energy and it flows through you. There are no limits to our potential and we can connect to the field of intention's energy when we are expressing our highest qualities.

To connect to this field, we need to imagine ourselves as we know we are. When we connect to who we really are, there is no division of any kind. For a look at our true nature, watch a group of toddlers. There is no division based on skin color, economic circumstance, ethnicity, religion, nationality, gender, ability, or anything else. They are all playing and enjoying the oneness of the experience and all they are. That is our true nature. It is only when the teachings of the world are forced upon us that the sense of separateness enters and causes conflict to occur in our lives.

We have all been subjected to that in one form or another by well-meaning parents, teachers, ministers, and governments. We develop a sense of "better than you, because…" We can continue to feel this way or we can let go of those thoughts, constructed by the ego, so that we can experience our highest feelings, those of joy, love, and compassion. It requires a conscious effort. That is communicating with the God of my understanding. Now I know that He is listening, He is answering, He is always there, at all time, in all ways, always. He is giving as I ask. I am not alone and my soul responds to my unity with my Source. The connecting is there all the time.

Anger has never served me, it has seldom done anything other than make me angrier; angrier that I could not control a situation, angrier that I could not get others to agree with me, just angrier. I now ask myself, "Would I rather be right or be happy?" I am choosing to be happy. I let the situation go. I consciously choose happiness and contentment over anger and control. My intent is helped along when, "the universe conspires to make it happen."

We make choices daily, choices about what we are going to wear, what we are going to fix for supper, and what errands we are going to do. Every minute of every day we have a decision to make that reflects who we are and how we are going to live. Why not choose our thoughts and feelings? We are only a choice away from contentment, peace, and happiness. One of the things I decided to do about a year ago involved television. I had been watching news more than I had in years. After the Super Tuesday Primary in 2012, I could see that all I was going to see until after the November election was going to be a barrage of negative political news. I quit watching news. I didn't listen to it on the radio and I didn't read the newspaper. I would occasionally see a newspaper headline or hear someone refer to an event, but I chose not to make it a part of my life. It was unbelievably relaxing to have media negativity removed from my daily life. Later in the year I decided to cancel my cable subscription and rely only on my choice of movies if I wanted to watch something on television. I do get some news from Facebook but I only read that which interests me concerning social or environmental issues that I choose to incorporate into my life.

Facebook has become a very important part of my journey to enlightenment. I have reconnected with former students, friends, and have made some incredible new friends. It has led me to some interesting "conversations." There have also been people who have an agenda and interests that I do not share. In some instances, they are benign and I just scroll right over them. Some of the issues that people express cause me to feel much negativity. In those cases, when it is a daily trend, I just remove them from my news feed. I do not get the posts that they send; hence, I do not have something negative to deal with and it works pretty well for me.

I have managed to connect with some incredible sites that offer much in the spiritual realm. There are sites that combine wisdom with artistry and photography and I find that I share a lot of these simply because they have so much to offer us all. I may be one of those irritating people to others and they can remove me from their news feed if that is the case. There is a list at the end of the book of the sites I have found to be so helpful.

CHAPTER THIRTY

Thirty years ago after going through a personally devastating divorce, I decided I would never remarry. I was thirty-one years old and not totally ready to give up on the fantasy of love. Shortly after that my six year detour came about. For the most part it was a time in my life that I treasure. When it was over, however, I was forty years old. I had children ages twelve and nine. The relationship had been my relationship and never involved the kids too much because I decided from the beginning it would never get to the marriage/family/happily ever after end. I just didn't realize at the time that it would last six years or that I would love and be loved in return. As a teacher, I had seen many blended families where the needs and desires of the parents' took precedence over the needs of the kids. I didn't want this for my children, nor did I want step-children.

When my relationship did end, I was starting a transfer to the science department of the middle school. Between the end of a relationship and a job transfer (both of which rank quite high on the list of stressful occurrences in life), all of my feelings of insecurity and worthlessness came bounding back big time. I was losing control of my life again, and I turned to the only thing I ever seemed to have control of, my drug of choice, food. I was tired of losing in life. Within the first year of teaching at the middle school, I had gained about sixty pounds and summer after that first year, I added another sixty. I was afraid I had something seriously wrong with me. I went to a doctor in Evansville and had a full battery of tests and blood work done. I had an extensive medical history taken. The doctor told me he felt I had a form of bulimia, sub-classed as "compulsive overeating." He recommended a counselor and I went. I began going to Overeater's Anonymous. I had always fought weight but had successfully lost about one hundred pounds with Weight Watchers when I was in my early twenties, before I was married and had kept the majority of it off for the ensuing twenty years. It was explained to me that all of my eating and dieting had finally caught up to me and my body was just tired of the struggle. I continued to gain until I reached three hundred seventy-five pounds. That weight, that fat body, protected me. It protected me from meeting anyone who could care for me, or profess to, then leave my life. It gave me the perfect reason to withdraw from life, and that is what I did. I lost some of the weight but still hovered anywhere from three hundred twenty-five to three hundred forty pounds for years. I said that I wanted to lose more weight, but I continued to eat in a way that would keep the pounds on.

I was a miserable individual. I remember vividly the first time I could not fit into a booth in a restaurant. I was with my friend, Ann, at a Dairy Queen for lunch after we had visited a nursery to buy some herb plants one spring. She was not embarrassed, but I was. I retreated further into my hermit phase of life. I developed high blood pressure. I had difficulty walking. My weight was debilitating, but it served me. This is difficult to write about because I remember thinking at the time that maybe God was using that time in my life so I would be a better person. I didn't judge others in quite the same way, not for the same reasons, but I was so filled with self-hatred that I did still judge. It was the only way I knew to feel even a little bit better about my life, to belittle other's choices. I was able to show my better qualities to Ann, but very few others. She showed me so much love, so much acceptance. It was not until three years ago after the birth of my second grandson, Gideon that I knew I would lose weight. A side bar to this story is that even though Carolyn and I had talked about getting together for years, I hadn't had the energy or confidence to let her see me in the physical condition I was in. Once the weight came off, I was ready to get out in the world again.

This was something that filtered through on my Facebook page that I felt was too good not to include. It was written by a thirty year old poet, Joanne Govure, from the Pacific Island of Nauru. It is entitled, *"Beautiful Prayer,"*:

I asked God to take away my habit.
God said, "No.
It is not for me to take away, but for you to give up."

I asked God to grant me patience.
God said, "No.
Patience is a by-product of tribulations. It isn't granted, it is learned."

I asked God to give me happiness.
God said, "No.
I give you blessings, happiness is up to you."

I asked God to spare me pain.
God said, "No.
Suffering draws you apart from worldly cares and brings you closer to me."

I asked God to make my spirit grow.
God said, "No.
You must grow on your own, but I will prune you to make you fruitful."

I asked for all things that I might enjoy life.
God said, "No.
I will give you life, so that you may enjoy all things."

I asked God to help me LOVE others, as much as he loves me.
God said....
"Ahhh, finally you have the idea."

We are given opportunities by God all the time. Whether we take these choices and create our lives productively is up to us. Words or ideas affect one's thoughts and that is our first step. Our thoughts affect how we feel. Those feelings affect our vibrations and our vibrations are what attract things to us.

Everything begins with a word. Consider Wilbur and Orville Wright. They began discussing flight. They probably discussed and drew out ideas for a flying machine. Their ideas, their thoughts, along with the intention to create a machine probably got them very excited. Even with machines that did not work as they had hoped, they kept their feelings positive, creating continued high vibration and they did indeed create the "first practical fixed-wing aircraft." Consider an alternative: they thought about a flight machine but dismissed it as a crazy idea or something they couldn't do and it went no further. If they possessed no intent to create a machine, the process would have stopped there. Or maybe, they made a couple of machines and got discouraged. The process would have stopped there. The point being, when the word (or idea) begins, it goes to a thought which affects your feelings, then your vibrations.

I don't believe for a moment that I had to 'suffer" for twenty years to learn any kind of lesson. I gave myself the words of "unlovable," "worthless," "not good enough." I thought those thoughts for years. Those words were what gave way to my thoughts. They gave me the food for the feelings I experienced and I got that which I attracted. When we fear life, we attract and experience what we fear. I asked, unconsciously, that I not be in another relationship where I could not release my fear of being hurt and that is just what I received. My asking was given in the form of a fat body. It is just that simple and I did not make those connections to my life until about a year ago. When Gideon was a baby and I made a specific, conscious decision filled with the intense desire to lose weight, I did and dramatically so!!

Nothing happens by coincidence or accident. We create our own reality. Nothing is ever done to us. We ask and we are given. We attract everything by our conscious or unconscious thoughts.

CHAPTER THIRTY-ONE

We can re-create ourselves minute by minute, day by day. This is exciting! Whatever we want to do, we can do. Whatever we want to be, we can become. Whatever we want to have can be ours. We can attract something consciously or unconsciously. When we do it unconsciously, events occur in our lives in a seemingly sporadic fashion and we don't understand why. When we realize that we are the ones responsible for all that comes to us in life, and that God is only answering our unconscious request, we can become more aware. We can then realize that we only need to give conscious attention to that which we desire and know that it will be given to us. This is the time to be thankful. It may not be as we envision it, nor in the time frame that we have in mine, but we can relax into the knowledge that when we place ourselves vibrationally in alignment with our Source, the essence of what we desire will be ours. Exciting, indeed!

Thoughts are what brings about the words, which brings our desires into fruition. Let's take a look at exactly how thoughts influence what happens in our life. We are of two minds. We have a subconscious mind that remembers everything and is what is creating our lives. It is the most powerful part of our mind. Then we also have the conscious mind which is divided into our conscious (aware) thoughts and our unconscious (unaware) thoughts. It is the conscious part of our mind that is responsible for telling the subconscious what to do.

The subconscious does some things automatically like remembering to breath, to cause us to scratch an itch, or all the workings of the body systems. The subconscious is always directed by the conscious part of our mind. When we are aware of the thoughts we are sending the subconscious, when we give them our conscious, undivided attention and we feel the feeling of already having achieved our desire, as Emerson stated, the universe "will conspire to make it happen." The subconscious has no other way to react. Because we are a part of God, His is the subconscious mind that allows for us to be the co-creator of our reality. It is His subconscious mind that is our subconscious mind. Everything in our lives can change according to our conscious desires. The two most powerful words that exist, "I am," are what defines us. Anything we put behind those words create the intent to be the very thing we envision. Our feelings that accompany these thoughts create the vibration needed to allow our desire to come to us, or not.

You may forget many things in life, but you are always conscious of "I am." After I read about the power of these two words, I noticed how I used them myself. I had become so accustomed to saying, "I am sick and tired of …" or, "I am so mad because…" When I did this, I was feeling negative and my life was reflecting this. When I made a simple change, "I am accepting," I am happy," "I am thankful for…," my experiences began to change. The former "I ams" gave me a bad feeling, whereas the later were encouraging. This is how you can tell, vibrationally, how closely you are aligning with your Source energy and with what you are manifesting in your life. If the vibrations are matching, you will feel good. If the vibrations are not in alignment, you will feel badly. It is a simple guide for you to know that you are allowing into your life that for which you have asked.

God belongs to no one religion. We all claim Him, as well we should, but not as individual members of certain religions or churches but rather as the Eternal Spirit within us all. Nothing comes from particles. There is only energy and energy is all we will ever be. It is what we are, pure vibrational energy. When we look at the color of one's skin, the set of one's facial features, or the clothes someone wears as different, we are separating ourselves, not only from each other but also from the source of which we are all a part. Does that mean diversity does not exist? Certainly diversity exists. Look at all the different flowers, trees, and animals. Diversity is wonderful, but not when it causes us to forget our oneness with it all. We are all the same, we are physiologically, on a cellular level, and spiritually sharing the oneness of our original creation. For us to reduce our humanity to these differences indicates we do not acknowledge the unity that is our birthright.

I have always enjoyed diversity. I remember a Sunday trip my family made to Spring Mill State Park, in southern Indiana, when I was about nine years old. The reason this particular visit stands out in my mind is because I met Tamika. My sister, cousin, and I were playing on swings, slides, and all the other things you find for kids to play on. A little Japanese girl about seven or eight timidly came up to the merry-go-round. I remember being so excited that I was going to play with someone from a whole different country. After realizing she didn't speak any English, we pointed to ourselves and said our names. She pointed to herself and said, "Tamika." I remember we all played, laughed, and had a wonderful time. I saw her uniqueness as a great thing. She spoke a different language, she was from a different country but somehow, at age nine, I was given a great gift. I saw that we were the same, kids who enjoyed playing together. I think because of that early experience and the way I have always viewed differences, I have been very luck. I have been able to accept some of the uniqueness of different individuals knowing that I have something in common with them. I still love to travel for the same reason, I can meet people from all parts of the United States or from Greece or from England, and enjoy the experience. I get to share in the wealth of their experiences which are different from mine, yet we are all the same and share similarities. I don't recognize differences as a bad thing. I don't understand the barriers we have put in place. We have come far from some of the barriers, but we have further to go. Some of the ideas the thoughts that serve to divide us are often generational, religious, national and racial. When we assume the values of any one group, it would serve us hold it up and ask the question in regards to our attitude, "Am I acting in a way that I would want them to treat me in this situation?" Many attitudes and beliefs, when held up to the light of that question, will crumble.

Cultural diversity and pride in our heritage is not a bad thing unless it serves to separate us. If we can truly celebrate the wondrous diversity in our universe without judging, criticizing, or condemning them then we can be united. All of these differences are similar to colors in a rainbow. We could not see the rainbow without all of the differences. The notes played by each of the instruments in an orchestra are needed to make the symphony. Humanity is not served if we expect everything to be the same. Every soul should sing their own song.

We are here to express our own idea of the very best we can be. How would we do that if all individuals were blonde-haired, blue-eyed, one hundred twenty-five pound women and brown0aired, brown-eyed, six foot two inch men who weighed one hundred eighty-five pounds? The point being that we couldn't. Just as surely as we have to know tall to know short, we must have a point of comparison in everything. In order to be all we can be, we have to be able to observe something then make a choice as to how we will relate to whatever it is we are observing. Just because we deem one thing as "bad" and the other as "good" doesn't necessarily make it so. We are simply using that information to help define who we are. Any man over six feet, two inches is considered tall. A six-foot, two inch man surrounded by professional basketball players appears short, it's a matter of perspective. What if we were to look at everything as a beautiful part of all that is? Everything is a part of the wondrous tapestry that gives us a chance to show kindness, to show compassion, and to allow us to be all we can be. A smile is a smile, a hug is a hug, and love is love in any language. Where is the separateness in that? On a spiritual level and on a cellular level, we all know this.

It is when the ego steps in that we experience difficulty. The ego says that a certain height, gender, nationality, and religious or political belief makes us a "better" person. If you are one of the "haves" you are therefore, better than the "have nots." It gets worse. We decide that because we are better, we know what is better for those whom we consider to be beneath us. Our goal is not to share our "betterness;" our goal is to edge ourselves even higher above them, just in case, mind you, they haven't figured out already that we have more. They must understand just how much better we are than they. The ego is always about "them" and "us." It is always about separating from oneness with everyone.

Where is the joy when we rob others of their joy? How can happiness, ours or theirs, be found when that is how we are forcing our soul to exist? How can peace and contentment ever be achieved? We need, for our own joyous life to occur, to remember that we are all one. Jesus said, "What we do to the least of these, my brothers, we do to ourselves." We are all one and we are all one with the higher source power. There is nothing that will ever separate us from that unity. We can forget it, we can ignore it, we can reject it, but it is as it is. When we depart from our physical bodies to our next great adventure and are reunited with all that is, we will be free once again. Our souls know this and that is why "stuff" is never enough to satisfy us. The only thing that will satisfy us is to give the ego its proper place and let it help define us, but not "run rampant like an unruly child." (Dalai Lama) Allow your thoughts and feelings to dwell on those aspects of life that create joy and love in your life.

CHAPTER THIRTY-TWO

Jesus was here to set an example of how we are to live our lives. He was here to represent God, as I feel we all are, because we are a part of that source power. He was here to show love to all he encountered. When we attend church services we are expressing the desire to be one with God.

If Sundays are the only day we express the best side of ourselves, we might want to re-examine our core beliefs. Many churches are "rich people churches" that seem to draw affluent citizens. They are "the" church to attend. Some attend to align themselves with a more affluent group of people than they associate with in their daily lives. Some like just like saying that they attend "such and such church" for the prestige it gives them. There again, the ego can cause people all sorts of problems. There are churches like that in Vincennes and there are churches in Anderson like that. There are churches and congregations like that everywhere. An elitist quality in a church goes against what is necessary to connect with Source.

God's grace covers everyone, period. I have read the Tao te Ching and found wisdom there. It is full of enlightenment about what I think of as ageless wisdom. I see the same enlightenment in what I know of the Bible. Buddhist teachings hold these truths also. I see enlightenment in the words of Emerson, Thoreau, and Shakespeare. I find the current words of Dr. Wayne Dyer, Eckhart Tolle, and Deepak Chopra full of wisdom and enlightenment. I find the lives of Mother Teresa and Princess Diana of Wales to have been lives that were polar opposites yet lives that exhibited great compassion. I find the life of Jimmy Carter, former president of the United States, can serve as a role model for us all as he continues to serve others internationally as a private citizen. The XIV Dalai Lama represents that essence of kindness and compassion that transcends any one religious belief. I find my inspiration in the words of Albert Einstein, Abraham Lincoln, Dr. Martin Luther King, Jr., Malcolm X, John Lennon, George Carlin, and many others. We become enlightened by reading with an open mind, listening to moving music, viewing beautiful works of art, and observing nature. We only need to look at some of the fractal patterns in nature, the beauty of a sunset, and the exuberance of a puppy to see God and let our souls free. God is everywhere; and, wherever I look, I am encountering God. I cannot help but be connected with my Source.

I go outside to my garden, see the dew on the plants, the immense oak, and the delicate butterflies and make that connection with the God of my understanding. I can imagine looking through God's eyes and viewing all of nature that exists and also saying, "It is good." If the eyes are the window to the soul that is what we all do when we appreciate nature.

CHAPTER THIRTY-THREE

It was in Dr. Dyer's PBS special that I first heard about the idea that if you wish to have a fulfilled life you need to, "think from the end." In other words, assume the feeling you would feel if you were already in possession of your desire. I wasn't quite sure how I could do this. Then I came across an inspirational post on Facebook that said, in effect, "Happiness is not something you achieve. In order to become happy, you have to "Be" happy." Happiness for any period of time has eluded me. If I could just for a moment choose to "Be" happy on my own, would I even recognize the feeling?

I was sitting on my deckio with a bottle of peach tea last summer. I was looking around, mostly at squirrels playing in my back yard. I was smiling and laughing because they were just having such a good time. I was right there with them. Out of a totally still day, the most wonderful breeze blew across the deckio and I literally caught my breath it felt so good. The only way I can come close to expressing it is that it was like a kiss from God telling me, "This is happiness, enjoy it." I continued to watch the squirrels and my enjoyment grew as I realized. "I am happy, truly, without a doubt, happy." It didn't take the man of my dreams, it didn't take going shopping, it didn't take winning the lottery, it didn't take anything but getting out of myself and immersing myself in the beauty of nature without any thoughts of anything other than those silly wonderful little squirrels doing squirrel things. This is happiness. I have had so many happy moments that I never acknowledged as happy. I was always looking for it but never finding it. All I ever had to do was simply connect with it and allow myself to just be happy.

"I am happy." Something else clicked inside during that experience. "I am" and the words that follow it are the most powerful words in the Universe. When I said that, they produced that which followed. I decided then and there that I was going to try saying that and other "I ams" to achieve the change I wanted.

I am generous.	I am non-judgmental.
I am kind.	I am non-condemning.
I am compassionate.	I am non-critical.
I am healthy.	I am abundant.
I am prosperous.	I am loving.
I am thankful.	

These have become my daily mantras. I say them before I drift off to sleep at night and I say them as I stumble to the shower in the mornings. I try to implement each quality daily. I find as time goes by there are more and more times to incorporate these. As I dwell on these, I no longer have time for my pessimistic thoughts. When they creep in, I replace them as quickly as possible with something more positive. There are only two emotions, fear and love. Am I coming from a place of fear and unruly ego or am I coming from a place of love and Source energy? I am consciously choosing; and in the choosing, I am experiencing the higher energy vibrations that connect me with my Source, or God. When I do that, I know I have connected with truth.

CHAPTER THIRTY-FOUR

What is truth and how do we find it? We find truth when there is no other answer. Your truths and my truths may be different, but they may represent a different place in terms of being somewhere on the sliding scale of polar opposites. Example: my "warm" may be your "hot" yet the temperature of the water is one hundred degrees. The hundred degrees represents actual truth, yet you and I are putting forth subjective truth in that it is subject to our bias of what we perceive as hot and cold. If the purpose of our lives spent in this tiny bit of time on Earth is to mean anything then we seek to find the "truth of the ages" so to speak. We seek to know the truths that set our soul free to live a satisfying fulfilled life. There is something more than just a day to day existence, we just need to know how to reach it. The more I got bogged down by life, the more I questioned and reached for something to bring me back up and out to a more pleasant experience. I looked to my surroundings, people in my life, current circumstances. I looked outward to find what can only be reached from within.

We are all given messages as we grow. If a child hears that he is clumsy and can't be expected to do well in a physical education class, doesn't that become his truth? Is it really truth? There are people who have lost limbs and are told they will never be able to participate in life as well as those with their limbs and they accept it as their truth and live a limited life. Then, there are others in this same circumstance who don't accept that as truth for themselves. They go on to face what seems to us to be insurmountable odds and go on to accomplish a fulfilled life. When we become aware that all of these messages may not really represent truth, we can examine them in the light and begin to question, "Who am I, really?" We can consciously decide what we are going to accept as our truth and that will lead us to who we really are and what kind of life we want for ourselves.

The truth will always be that of love, for yourself and for others. When we are trying to consciously make a decision, we can always ask ourselves, "What would love do?" What you do for others, you do for yourself. What you do for yourself, you do for others. This comes from love because there are no others, we are all one with Source. You can then look at everyone you meet and see them as a reflection of yourself. We are all the same, all physical life, everything on this planet has the same cellular signature of God. We come from the same energy that created everything, we are the energy, the part of it and the whole of it. There is nothing but that which is. I commented on a Facebook post to a friend's post and he wrote back, "Wait until you look through the eyes of God into the eyes of God and have God look back at you. You will connect with people in a different way."

Most of us spend our time here on earth feeling that we are being batted about like a ball in a pinball machine. We think that circumstance dictate and define what happens to us. We do not realize that we are attracting everything into our lives; that is law. We accept that there are "forces" out there, some kind of order to the chaos but often can't quite seem to grasp it. We see it as children when we go chasing after fireflies and finding them so miraculous that they have those tiny little light bulbs on them. We know it when we lay on our backs looking at the patterns of the clouds as they drift by. We know it when we pet a kitten or tumble with a puppy. When we are children, we can even smell fragrance in a dandelion. As we age, we let the opinions of others tame our natural instincts and wonder why life gets drab.

When the Bible tells us that to get into heaven we must become as little children, this is a reminder that when we were children we saw glory and magnificence in everything. We loved everyone, we didn't see anything as separate from us. We accepted everything fully, we didn't judge. To accept truth as a child is to live a joyous life and know that all is joy. That is why Heaven is right here, right now.

With God, all things are possible, for everyone. This leaves out nothing. So, why do we sometimes feel that our prayers are not answered? There are several reasons. I used to ask in a begging way as though God might not answer. While I asked, I wondered if there were any kind of deal I might be able to strike with Him that might make my plea come true. Therein lies part of the problem. I was asking for something with my preconceived outcome on my time frame, on my terms., I said that I believed God was powerful enough to give it to me but that He could use my request, deny it, and punish me for past deeds by not giving it to me. He gives in accordance with our thankfulness for the prayer already being answered, to the degree we have faith that it is answered, and the clarity with which it is asked.

When we ask, verbally in prayer, or in thought of what we desire, the God in us, our subconscious mind, begins working the universe in a way that will have our desires met and sometimes we wonder what if it doesn't happen? This sends a message of lack and doubt. The subconscious mind then shifts to this new request and starts putting the universe in order to get "lack" delivered to us. We go back and forth with our actual requests. We think we have asked for one positive thing but our attention and vacillation between the having and the not having may very often result in nothing happening. We then feel as though we have been denied that for which we have asked. If we cannot be clear in what we want, how can God know what to send our way?

Some of the time our prayers involve those who are ill or dying. We want someone to live, so that is what we pray for. We don't want them to suffer so we are, quite naturally, conflicted. What we rarely take into consideration is the desire of the person we are praying for. Wanting to die is not considered okay by our society.

Our soul is free and eternal, it never dies. Sometime, when you are with a loved one, they will send you to get a meal or send you home and when you return they have passed through the door from this room into another. We beat ourselves up that we weren't there but in truth, it would have made no difference. Their soul was ready to leave the physical body. Our souls don't view death as our ego does. Our soul knows only love. It is our egos that use fear and death synonymously. The soul doesn't see itself as giving up anything or leaving anything because it understands that we are all one for all time. It is our egos that fear death. We grieve that we will never be able to hug that person again, talk with them or share laughter with them. We will miss them and we will grieve. When my mother was ill, a friend advised me to be sure and let her know that it was okay for her to go when she needed to go. She said that was the one thing that she and her sisters had not done for their mother. I listened to her and I told my mother that. I am very glad I did. It did not change the outcome but I think it gave us both peace. I was with my mother when she passed on. I was holding her as she took her last breath. I was able to say good-bye as her essence left her body. I could feel a difference as it happened. That was almost fifteen years ago and the experience dispelled much of the fear I had about death. Any doubt I had about the existence of a soul was gone. Since I have been reading and thinking and understanding about our oneness with God, I realize what a great gift this was. I know now that her soul had been "fighting the fight" and was ready to go back to the place from whence it came, and did. I still miss her physical presence and always will.

CHAPTER THIRTY-FIVE

What is our purpose for being here? I am not sure my grandparents asked that question, I think they spent their life on purpose. Raising children, working a farm, cooking for the farm hands who came to help bale the hay, feeding chickens and milking cows, gardening and canning so there would be food on the table in winter, they lived a very purposeful life and realized it. We ask this question because we have the time to ask it. If we were involved in connecting with others, with serving others, whether it is gardening and canning, easing the lives of AIDS patients, or fixing cars, would we have time to wonder what our purpose is? No, we would be living our purpose.

Sometimes we downplay the importance of our existence. Our ego tries to convince us that what we are doing is unimportant unless it makes us a lot of money or brings us fame. No one is here by accident. Our purpose is not so much about what we do as it is about how we feel about what we are doing. As a teacher for thirty-four years, I often questioned my purpose. I felt disempowered to make changes and truly impact students' lives. Education became more of an assembly line of nine month spans where you knew you were sending kids unprepared to face the next assembly line. Had I only been able to see what I had to offer each of those children; how much richer all our lives would have been. I do know that teaching was my purpose in life. It was a choice I made daily even when I wished for a snow day to give me a break in the long days of winter, and even when I cursed the educational system itself.

If you have not recognized your purpose, it will find you. Your purpose is what you are, not what you do. It is knowing, "this is who I am" (those two words again). It doesn't always need to be locked into an occupation. Your purpose can be found when you sing, when you change diapers or when you are playing tennis. It is found when you know you are where you belong. That state of knowing where you belong can be taken one step further if you introduce servitude into the equation. If you love tennis, share that love with others in some way, and you will elevate your purpose. There is a saying, "Do not die with your music still in you." Live the life you were meant to live and never be concerned that it is too late, it never is. You have experienced what you have experienced, when you have experienced it, to lead you to where you are right now, and that is exactly where you need to be in this moment. Accept that and you realize that you are already living your life "on purpose."

Reflecting on my life and how my experiences fit together to get me where I am today, I consider my career in education. It was always what I thought I wanted from the time I was very young. Remember that back in the 1950s, there were not as many options to females that there are today. If you went to college then, it was usually to be a teacher or a nurse. There were some brave women who pursued other careers, but many fields weren't open like they are today. When I was in college I went into elementary education for my major because that is what my mother wanted. After some psychology classes I really wanted to go into psychology. My parents thought it would be a career with few opportunities. My mother, a teacher herself, wanted me to get my degree in education so that I would always have "something to fall back on." I could have gone on to pursue a degree in psychology after my degree in education, but I didn't. I was tired of school, I was ready to get on with my life. My destiny was education, not psychology. Sometimes I can't help but wonder, "what if," but spending time reviewing your choices is an exercise in futility. If at any time in our life we regret our choice of career, we can decide to change it. If it is a different choice you make with the intent to change, then doors will be opened to make it your reality. Do not let others tell you about your own purpose. If you don't feel that a path is one you want to traverse, then follow another one. Your purpose is yours alone. We should not presume to know what is best for others, but we often do. Listen to your heart. That is where you will find the core of your soul. Invite what brings a sense of joy into your heart daily. Buddhist wisdom states that, "There is no way to happiness, happiness is the way." Living a purposeful life is found in bringing purpose and joy to everything you do.

The more I read about the importance of awareness and the importance that our consciousness plays in ordering our life, the more interested I become in meditation. Nature provides me with the best venue for this. I could sit on the deckio in the summer, close my eyes and feel the warmth of the sun and totally submerge myself in the warmth. Once the weather got cooler, that no longer worked. I would then just look out upon the day and take in all the magnificence of the trees, birds, squirrels, and whatever the day offered and that works too. I realized that although quiet is good, we can meditate anywhere for even short periods of time. We can meditate in the shower being aware of the warm drops of water raining down on our body and washing our cares down the drain. I can also meditate myself into a great feeling with a wondrous piece of music. It is the intent of gaining the feelings of love, happiness, joy, and peace that creates a meditative state and that is different for everyone. Whatever makes your soul sing is your form of meditation.

I had the opportunity to go to a workshop on "Connecting with your Inner Wisdom," given at the Unity Universalist Church in Anderson. There were five steps involved and the first week we had the introduction and the first two steps. We were to practice the week following our first meeting then come back in a week to share our experiences and get the last three steps. I practiced these first two steps and found I had no thoughts. I thought I would hear inspirational music or see bright colors or something, but I got nothing. When I went back the second week, those who shared their experiences were very interesting. I raised my hand and said that I had no thoughts, after two or three minutes of nothingness I then just started thinking about how much time was left and I would open my eyes and look at the clock. I was assured there was no right or wrong to it. The third step was to ask our Inner Wisdom to tell us what she had for us in a non-verbal way. I still got nothing. No cymbals, no flash of light, no animal totems, nothing. The fourth step was to ask her to reveal the message verbally. Oh, well, here we go again. By this time we were up to about a ten minute period of time because when we got the message we were to open our eyes, write it down, then close our eyes again. I waited and waited, finally I asked, "Please send me something…" Then I noticed the buzz of a light fixture about me. It continued to buzz and I thought of a bee. I opened my eyes and wrote down, "Bee." That was it. We then completed the fifth step and as we were getting ready to share and I looked that the word "Bee" it hit me… it isn't "bee," it's "be." My inner wisdom was communicating…maybe.

Later that evening, the first message that popped up as I checked Facebook was one from an inspirational site I had "liked." It read, "If we become our thoughts, like the Buddha says we do, what happens when we think no thoughts?" Wow, it was as though I had written the question. I hit the comments to see what people had to say. The first comment said, "You enter oneness. Your mind releases all resistance and you attract and become nothing but pure positive energy." Some of the other comments were: "No thoughts, no ego," "Enlightenment. We become," "We become everything." "Be" and the last one…. "I AM."

There are no coincidences. This message was exactly what I needed to answer my question. I realized that for meditation to work for me, I was going to have to get out of the mind-set that it was going to have to happen a certain way. If we leave ourselves open to communication, it will come to us. Any experience that leads us to our highest feelings of kindness, compassion, love, and joy, are the feelings that will create the highest vibration, align with Source, and attract the essence of what we desire into our life. Any experience that leads to frustration, despair, and anger are of lower energy, lower vibration, and do not represent truth. Meditation is one of the ways of gaining access to the highest feelings we are capable of at any given time.

CHAPTER THIRTY-SIX

When I began to read and research, "abundance" kept coming up. I always thought "money" when I saw the word "abundance." I like money, I like it a lot. It pays my bills and lets me get stuff. It lets me buy stuff for my kids and grandkids. It is fun to have and spend. It allows me to travel and have really great experiences. I was never particularly good at saving it because I couldn't see any point in having it hang around in a bank. My parents always tried to point out how good it was to have something "put back for a rainy day." Like many other things they tried to get me to do, it was one that just never really took. The message behind it, that of lack (save now for a time when there isn't enough), that message stuck.

I always imagined winning the lottery and what I would be able to do with all that money. It never involved putting a lot in the bank. Of course, some would go there because I would have to put it somewhere before I spent it. I had lofty goals of donating huge amounts to needy causes. I didn't imagine a big house or expensive cars. I thought about all the other people I would gift with a million dollars. Just dreaming about spending it was probably more fun than actually getting it. In actuality, I seldom buy lottery tickets. It's just that my thoughts about money were at the forefront of manifesting a fulfilled life.

After reading *The Moses Code* and learning of the power of the words "I am," I would repeat, "I am abundant," "I am wealthy," "I am prosperous." As I continued to read about the flow of abundance and think of the word as it applied to life, rather than money, something shifted inside me. It wasn't a sudden awakening. It was just a shift in my thinking that cause me to know, deep down inside, that I AM abundant, in the truest sense of the word. There is an abundance of good in the world, of sun, of rain, of air, of nourishment, and yes, of money. There is enough for all of us. The ego often keeps us in a state of need. We are never good enough, smart enough, pretty enough and we never have enough. The ego would have us believe that there is a shortage of everything. The truth is, there is only abundance in the world. There is an abundance of everything, if we will allow it to flow to us, and through us to others, there will be enough for everyone. I no longer look at dollars, I look at my experiences and see how they reflect abundance in all things. It is such a blast of freedom from doubt and worry.

In the very last moment of life in the physical realm, we won't be concerned about the money we have in the bank, we will be thinking of those we love and have loved. When we express thanks for all we have now, we see that we are so very abundant. If we are giving our thanks, we are acknowledging that we have these things in our lives. After you gaze at the stars at night and feel the immense, abundant, magnificent universe whining of our scarcity seems silly. All of life is relative and this is one of the greatest gifts of all. When we place our egotistical desire for "more, more, more" in relationship to the universe, it becomes insignificant. When we understand the flow of abundance, we see that when one person has abundance in their lives, it keeps it from no one else. It would be like my saying, "Oh, I have been healthy for ten years, so I am going to be sick for two years to give someone else a chance to be healthy." Abundance and well-being are both the natural flow in our lives. It is only when we resist them, or perceive lack or illness that we do not receive them. All that God knows is abundance and well-being. We are the ones who perceive lack and thus resist the flow of abundance into our lives. We will achieve abundance when we acknowledge that abundance is everywhere and allow it to flow to us and through us.

It wants to flow. If we hoard money and are greedy with it, the flow will stop. If we accept it, allow it, and not become too attached to it, then it will continue to flow through us. Do you know there are something like three billion pennies tossed away each year? That is thirty million dollars, tossed away, ignored. Do you pick up a penny? Anytime we leave money on the ground, because it is too insignificant in our minds to bother with, we are not acknowledging and accepting the flow of abundance to us. We are ignoring and turning down the abundance that is flowing. If you pick up that penny, send out a thanks and acknowledge it as part of the abundance in your life, you are allowing even more come your way.

CHAPTER THIRTY-SEVEN

The XIV Dalai Lama says, "Do not use the teachings of Buddha to become a Buddhist, use the teachings of Buddha to make you become better at whatever you believe." You have to love and respect a religion that does not try to convert and whose practices center on selflessness while promoting kindness and tolerance of all people. Anytime we find inspirational thoughts that serve to unite rather than separate us, we need to make them part of our lives.

There are numerous American Indian pieces of wisdom that are ageless. An example of this is from Chief Seattle, leader of the Squamish Indians in the American Northwest, who stated in 1854, "Humankind has not woven the web of life. We're but one thread within it. Whatever we do to the web, we do to ourselves. All things are bound together. All things connect."

The *Tao te Ching*, written by the prophet Lao Tzu five hundred years before the birth of Jesus, contains some of the same teachings that Jesus shared. When the wisdom crosses the reaches of time, that repetition is leading us to truth. God is always talking to us but if we think that the messages from God will come to us in a certain way, we won't always hear it.

God lives in the realm of the absolute. We live in the realm of the relative. For God to experience magnificence, it was necessary for a world and a system to be created whereby He could know himself experientially. God wanted to experience himself. The energy that was Source simply created all there is. It is waiting to be physically made manifest. There is only oneness and one can't be divided. In God's realm nothing exists in relation to anything else. All there is in God's world is love. There is no death because life goes on forever, is infinite and is eternal. This is what our spirit is part of. In the physical world of the relative there is duality (hot/cold) and the law of Cause and Effect. Since God is love, He can't also be fear. If God is the source of everything then He has no needs including the need to punish us. When we speak of judgment, who would God have to judge if we are perfect in His eyes, just as we are. If the oneness is God and God is good and can't be divided and we are part of that, then the purpose of our life is not to be apart from any of it.

Diversity is a great thing. Like everything else in life, it can be positive or negative depending on your thoughts and feelings about it. The diversity of cultures is wonderful. The diversity of music from all parts of the world, the artwork from all time and places of the world are all different, but beautiful And the food – Greek, French, Italian, Cajun – all of the different culinary feasts that each culture contributes to the whole make a wondrous delicacy. The chefs, artists, and musicians are all one. They share joyous emotions while they are co-creating. Those are the joyous emotions we all share as one. If diversity is used as an excuse to keep people separate from each other, to use their uniqueness as a wedge to come between us, then diversity isn't so great. It would be boring, indeed, if we were all the same.

Is a rose better than a daffodil? They both have different seasons of bloom, different shapes, different colors and different fragrances. They are two of our most loved flowers and they are both enjoyed because of those differences. They are loved for their strength and what they both contribute to our gardens. A garden wouldn't be the tapestry it is if there were only roses or only daffodils, neither would we have the chance to live the life we choose if we had nothing to choose from. If God had wanted everything to be the same, He would have created it so. He wanted us each to be able to experience life in a unique way. No one other person on the planet is exactly like me. Although I am unique, I am also one with every other living thing on the planet. The joy we seek in life is not found if we try to be the same as everyone else. True joy comes when you recognize and celebrate your individuality.

CHAPTER THIRTY-EIGHT

The whole idea of the immensity of the Universe is rather interesting. Our entire Solar System spins at one hundred thirty-four miles per second in the outer orbit of the Milky Way Galaxy. There are over two hundred billion stars in the Milky Way galaxy and as many as six billion of those have planetary systems like our sun does. That huge, immense Milky Way Galaxy is only one of the one hundred twenty-five billion galaxies in our visible universe. Keep in mind that these facts are only the known information about the visible part of the universe which indicates that the numbers could be even more astounding as technology improves.

We are energy and consciousness. It is our conscious thoughts that direct the energy so that we become co-creators in the formation of matter that is in the physical manifestation of our desires. The thoughts that are given our attention become our reality. Words, our ideas, become thoughts. Those thoughts when dwelled upon create a vibrational frequency that will either allow or resist our desire. Giving unwavering attention to a thought means that we have to be aware that whenever we share our desires with someone they may very well tell us we're crazy or tell us why none of this "manifesting stuff" is to going to work. This problem is easily solved by sharing your desires only with your source. When you have an idea of something you desire to do, or to have, a desire for some goal in your life, think about it, know that the essence of it will be given to you and keep yourself in the best feeling place you can, to allow it to come into your life. Do not harbor doubt, do not think about all the ways this can't work, don't think of how you will deal with "failure." If you do those things, you are offering a resistance to what is flowing to you. Be thankful, spend your time anticipating getting what you have asked for. Have faith and believe. Your thoughts and feelings will align vibrationally with that desire that you wish to attract. This happens, good or bad, whether we realize it or not at the time.

This past holiday season I had the house decorated, packages wrapped and was listening to Christmas music that my son had transferred from his computer to my phone. One of the songs was "Christmas in New Orleans." I loved it and danced around when it came on, I wanted to be there. I was looking forward to another trip down there sometime in 2013. I called Carolyn one day to chat and see how things were going in her life. She said that she was going to Sandy's for Christmas. I laughed and asked her if she would like some company. I ended up spending Christmas in New Orleans. I had not consciously drawn this into my life at the time, but my vibrations had aligned with the desire to return to New Orleans and the opportunity was given to me. See how the Law of Attraction works? When we can place ourselves in a highly vibrational state, we attract abundance, well-being, and unforeseen opportunities. Good things will come to us. I pictured myself there again with no worrying or placing conditions on the how and when and it became my reality.

Worries, concerns, and doubts expressed in any way are going to introduce negative experiences into our lives or will disallow positive experiences. The longer and more frequently we are in a place of highest vibrations of love, joy, gratitude, and compassion, the better our life experiences will become. It cannot work any other way.

Another thing I noticed as I began to think differently was that when I used "I am" followed by the characteristic of what I wanted to become, it worked. It was pretty difficult to repeat, "I am non-judgmental" several times a day without becoming extremely aware of all the judging I was doing. I have never thought of myself as a prejudiced individual. When I think of prejudice, I think of it as relating to a group of people. If you think of it in its truest sense, that of "pre-judging" then we can understand that it applies no only to groups but also individuals. We judge others because we judge ourselves. Our ego encourages us to judge so that "others" can be put where they belong so that we can continue to feel superior. We judge out of fear and find ourselves and others worthy of our criticism. It is only when we quit judging ourselves and others that we can allow our light to shine. We come to appreciate that which we are and have no reason to pass judgment on another. When you can look in the mirror and no longer see the flaws but see what God sees – a perfect soul – you have reached the place where there is no longer any reason to judge. When you can do that, the rest of life becomes much easier. Learning not to judge myself critically is something I work on daily.

"Life is a courageous journey or nothing at all. We cannot become who we want to be by continuing to do exactly what we've been doing. Choose to listen to your inner voice, no jumbled opinions of others," says John Townsend. Albert Einstein said that we cannot solve our problems using the same thinking that created them. Just as our thoughts in the past have created our life as we know it today, our thoughts today shape our future "nows." What thoughts you accept and which thoughts you dismiss become extremely important if you want to see your life change. If you are already leading a fulfilled life, you have been putting these principles into action already. What we dwell on is attracted to us. We are energy; energy vibrating in response to our emotions. Like vibrations attract like vibrations according to the Law of Attraction. If our thoughts are fear-based, our emotions will be negative and have a low vibrational frequency and we will attract experiences that reflect that. If our thoughts are love-based, our emotions will be positive and have a high vibrational frequency and we will attract positive experiences.

CHAPTER THIRTY-NINE

I lead a solitary life. I am retired, I have lived in this community for four years. I have made many wonderful friends but they are involved with jobs and their own families. I don't have a life with people popping in and out or calls to go for coffee or lunch. That kind of life may only exist in my fantasy world anyway, because I don't know of anyone who lives like that. My son and his young family have a full and busy life. We get together when we can, but I don't depend upon them to be my entertainment. I garden alone unless there is Master Gardener project that several of us get involved with. I quilt and read, both solitary activities. While I love people, most of my life has been spent pursuing activities that are not group or team oriented.

One thing I usually do in the morning is to check Facebook while I'm fixing coffee and breakfast. I am always finding something interesting on there. I am sure that Andrew might say it is because I have "liked" some "Woo-Woo" sites. This morning I found something I had never considered: "If an alien in a galaxy sixty-five million light years away is looking at us through a telescope, right now, they would be looking at dinosaurs." Wow!! That started me thinking about the time-space continuum again. Now, you and I both know that we are here and dinosaurs are long gone. If those aliens boarded a spacecraft and came toward us, they would have kind of a motion picture of the evolution, or development, of life on

Earth because by the time they got here, they would arrive on the Earth as it is now. Time is what allows reality to exist. Reality changes as our thoughts change. We can literally create what we want the future "now" to be. If our thoughts remain as they are, things will still change, but the direction of that change will continue as it is now. For humankind to impact the creation of a different planet, we will need to change the direction of our thoughts and consciously choose thoughts that vibrate with love, joy, kindness, and compassion. The vibrations of those qualities will send out a ripple effect. If enough people shift their thoughts and feelings, it can be felt worldwide. It is said that on a scale of zero to one thousand, the average person is in a vibrational range of two hundred. If we work and raise our vibrational level to five hundred that increased energy could impact up to ninety thousand people. The higher your vibrations, the more the ripple effect will take place and the more people will benefit. I am not sure where I would fall on that particular vibrational scale but I hope it is doing some good.

What works for us and what doesn't work? The first time I went to the casino in New Orleans, I was with friends and having a good time. I experienced some winning and some losing. The winning seemed better, but in this particular experience, losing was okay too. In life it is this way as well. When we are enjoying the entire experience we don't consider the winning or losing aspect of it. We enjoy the doing and being aspects. It is when winning at anything becomes the most important part of the experience that things become problematic. This is because in our desire to win we often concentrate more on losing and fear losing. Our thoughts can change our perspective which can, in turn, change our experience. Winning and losing at the casino can become totally a matter of how you want to think and feel about it.

Let's say we go to the casino with one hundred dollars. As you play the machines, keep track of your play. If I play for an hour and accumulate one hundred thirty points, that means I have actually played six hundred fifty dollars through the machines. If I go home with fifty of my original one hundred dollars that could mean one of two things – depending on which way you want to think about it. I could say I lost fifty dollars and come out a bit depressed because I had "lost" fifty dollars. Or, I can choose to view it differently. I played six hundred fifty dollars through the machines and walked out with fifty dollars. Somewhere I had to have won six hundred dollars or I could not have played that much money through the machines. I leave as a winner. Yes, that play had cost me some of my money, but I was winning as I played, a fact that we often overlook at casinos and in life also. This applies to all of life. "It's what you look at that matters, not what you see," said Thoreau. If you constantly see yourself winning, you will maintain a more positive outlook on everything and winning in all things will be drawn to you. If you see everything as losing, then that is what will continue to be attracted. If we come out of any experience with more understanding of who we are, we come out a winner.

If we bless a situation, rather than cursing it, we come out ahead. We make a statement about who we are in all situations by the way we react to them. Our thoughts and reactions about situations shape not only that situation but also future situations and who we become as a result. Our perceptions of occurrences in the "now" of our own reality can be influenced by our thoughts at any given time.

CHAPTER FORTY

From Wikipedia, I found that there are 2,870 religions in the world. If we are of the thought that our religious beliefs are what will get us into heaven, and if each of those religions espouse a particular path as being the only way, then how can you know which one is the right one? If we take the top five religions, and the number of followers – Christianity, 2.1 billion – Islam, 1.2 billion – Hindu, 785 million – Buddhism 360 million – Judaism 17 million – that is 4.4 billion of the nearly 7 billion people on earth accounted for. Thirteen percent, or about another 800 million, consider themselves either Atheist or non-religious. Now our total is a little over 5 billion. This leaves about 2 billion people fitting somewhere into the remaining 2800+ religions. This seems to be an incredible number of groups of people who think they have the answer about how to get to paradise. It gets crazier when we look at Christianity. Of the 2 billion Christians, a little over half are Catholic (which considers itself to be the one True church). According to UN statistics, the protestant half of Christians may have as many as 22,000 denominations and maybe as high as 35,000. There are a lot of people seeking answers and there are a lot of groups claiming to have the answer.

This indicates a lot of separateness, even within the major religion of Christianity. What if none of it matters? If God has no favored people, if He is love, unconditional love, then all of the religions are covered, all people are equally important to Him, and all of the people in those groups, including the Atheist and non-religious, will be welcome. We are all a part of his creation, He favors no one person over another. He loves us all, we will all be welcome. We are a part of God and God is everywhere and that means there is no place He is not. Can it ever be, then, that any of us can not be a part of that which is God?

CHAPTER FORTY-ONE

My parents were both very strong-minded eldest children. My dad was the oldest of four children, three boys and a girl. One of the boys died when he was young. His sister was the youngest, moderately mentally handicapped and lived with my grandmother. We were not at all close to my dad's family and I found out more about his family after he passed away than he had ever shared with us. Although his dad died when I was six months old, I regret never having the experience of getting to know the kindness of my grandmother that other people shared with me. I only saw the cold woman that my mother viewed and accepted that as my own view.

My mother was raised in an alcoholic household with a strong-willed, verbally abusive father. My mammaw was a quiet woman and I loved her more than anyone else in the whole world. As an adult, my mother's desire to control her own family came about because she had no control over her own family life during her formative years. Mother went to college and became a teacher when most women got married out of high school. She was twenty-nine and my dad was twenty-eight when they married. I came along four years later and my sister three and one-half years after that.

From the time I was born, I've had a mind of my own and have been very "head-strong" – which is a nice way to say "stubborn." Fear of punishment served well to keep me controlled as I grew up. I don't remember spontaneous hugs from either of my parents unless we got hurt. There were hugs and kisses at bedtime but other than that, nothing I recall. I also do not remember much laughing or fun. Part of that, I think, is the time and place in which I was born. Everyone had their jobs and chores to do and there wasn't a lot of time left for fun. We did go on Sunday afternoon drives and I remember always looking forward to those.

When I was born no one told me I was to be mild-mannered and obedient. This caused me an inordinate number of problems. It was only compounded when my sister was born. Someone clued her in. So we have an older stubborn child with a mother who is going to win that battles and a younger sister who is quiet and obedient. As I grew older, I exercised control of my life in one area only – that of food. Studies have shown that in cases of abusive substances, whether it is food, drugs, or alcohol, the addictive personality is very strong willed. Society sees it as a problem of no "will-power." Actually, the opposite may be the case. Both times in my life when I lost major amounts of weight, over one hundred pounds each time, it was when I was willing to give up the control that food had over me that the weight losses occurred. In both cases, as I review it now, I can see that was what happened. When you surrender the need to control, the substance that is really controlling your life, no longer does and the problem can be worked out. I am not saying that this is easy to do. It isn't easy, but the reward is so much greater than the problems we create as we keep that need to control going full force.

Another way that we can look at what we perceive as disappointing aspect of our life is to think about why is isn't working. What is there about any situation that we find unacceptable? When we ask that, we need to follow it by asking, "What are the acceptable parts of the situation?" Sometimes we are just on auto-pilot. We are letting our subconscious mind take control of our thoughts, our feelings, and our lives. We react as we have always reacted to every circumstance, even when our blood pressure continues to go up or when we are turning to food or drugs. Our negativity affects our body by bringing us illnesses that we would otherwise not be experiencing. When we shift our thoughts, we can often self-correct physical conditions that cause us grief. I think this may be one of the reasons meditation is suggested so often. It is a different way of approaching our thoughts. It is a new experience so we don't have that auto-pilot kick in. Anytime I go within – to my feelings – the more easily I can tap into feelings that are better vibrationally. If we send out a silent "thank you" when we reach those places of better feelings, that act of giving thanks is like a catalyst for the good feelings to stay longer. The more thankful we can be, the more experiences find their way to us to give more for which to be thankful. It really does work like that.

Another important component in attracting the essence of what we desire is our intent. Our focused intent toward our desire gives fuel to our positive thought and feelings. If we don't have intent, we are only daydreaming. I can look around my house and if I desire a clean house, I cannot keep looking at the clutter and expect to get up the next morning and find a clean, straightened house. If my goal is to have a clean house and I do nothing, then my intent is to continue to have a dirty house. When your intent aligns with your desire, you will find the time and energy to act. If you have deep cleaning, moving furniture, etc. in mind, you will find the help you need to be successful – if that is your true intent. Because we are vibrational beings, it is only necessary for our intent to align with our desire. When our intent does not align with our desire we use what are called excuses for why our desire is not met. If you tell your friends that you plan on going to the driving range to improve your golf swing, then you don't go, realize that it is not your intent. You are satisfied using the "no time to go to the driving range" excuse for your golf swing to remain as it is. The Law of Attraction is real, but it is not a magic panacea for all your experiences in your life. If you dwell on the messy house or the poor golf swing, that is what you will get. It is when the intent matches with the desire vibrationally that you will attract the essence of what you truly desire. The degree to which your attention is given to your feelings about your desire is the degree to which you will align with that desire. The less you resist, the sooner your desire will come to you.

CHAPTER FORTY-TWO

Feelings and attitudes about our circumstances are very important. The realization of our desires, however, begins with our thoughts. We have the subconscious mind that literally runs our life. It monitors the beat of our heart, causes us to jerk away when there is an object thrown at us and causes us to scratch our head when it itches. It controls things automatically. This is the wonderful part of the subconscious. But the really great thing is that it can also be programmed to give us the essence of what we desire. Think about when you learned to drive. You consciously went step by step, check mirror, put car in reverse, back out of the garage, put turn signals on and slow down for upcoming stop sign, look both ways, carefully turn, etc. Your conscious mind was giving all of this information to your subconscious mind. It readily accepted it and stored it. After a while you simply got in the car and without consciously giving the orders to the subconscious it took over and you were able to drive without giving it any thought. The subconscious mind does exactly what the conscious mind tells it to do. This is also why a certain fragrance can instantly remind us of someone or some event. It is programmed in the subconscious. When we become aware of our thoughts we can program the subconscious the way we want to, rather than having it happen with random thoughts. We have to give new messages to the subconscious mind that will override the messages already there. Positive thoughts and messages will override negative thoughts and messages because they are operating at a higher vibration. If we can assume the feelings of already having our desire, the subconscious will react to that and it will work to that end. If we introduce doubt, the subconscious will react to that new directive. You will be letting your conscious awareness give the messages you want to your subconscious. Like vibrations attract like vibrations: therefore, if we are wanting good things to come to us, we have to have those good feelings as that will align us vibrationally to our desire. Thomas Edison said, "Opportunity is missed by most people because it is dressed in overalls and looks like work." Accept all opportunities sent your way to help you achieve your desires and realize that it may require some effort on your part to make it happen. The Law of Attraction is not like a "twitch of the nose" that gave Samantha what she wanted on "Bewitched."

Another portion of attracting what we want into our lives is by getting the feeling of already having it. I had to think about how that worked. If we believe first, then we will see the results. This goes against all we seem to experience. When we're thinking in this way, we have to ignore everything that we see and hear that is contrary to what we wish to achieve. We have to get to the point where we ignore what has happened in the past, whatever our ego tells us is not possible, and whatever shred of evidence that goes against what we want. It requires imagination that goes beyond daydreaming. It is basically total faith without doubt ever being accepted into your thoughts. It is about knowing that God wants for you and will give you what you ask for.

Another aspect of attracting into our lives that which he desire it to know that we never get what we "want." When we think "want," we are acknowledging lack, something we don't have. If we feel there is a lack; then it is lack that the subconscious mind will give us. The law of Attraction is always working but it works very specifically if we are going to achieve that which we desire. We must be aware of how it works. This is once again where our thoughts and feelings can help. I wanted to sell the duplex but it was not until I felt the feelings of having achieved it, not the feeling of wanting the sale to close, that the achievement of the goal was realized. If you concentrate on the fact that you don't have something – that is exactly what you will get, the "not having." There is a lot to consider when we think about the Law of Attraction but it will come together eventually.

The details are unimportant. For the Law of Attraction to work for us, we are not to be concerned with anything other than a clear desire and vibrational alignment. The Universal subconscious mind (or Source) is working to give us what we have asked for. Maybe for that wish to be fulfilled we will need an influx of cash. That influx may be in the form of a chance at a temporary part time job. We cannot overlook any opportunity that presents itself and write that off because it was not the way we had envisioned it, therefore it isn't valid. We have to be open to all possibilities of achieving our desire. Belief without a doubt, faith without question regardless of anything you see or hear in your outward world, and quiet thankful patience, and you will get it. Let the Universe work out the details, the time span for this to occur and the way in which it will happen. Don't set yourself up for doubt and resistance by expecting it to come on your time schedule and in a certain way. Just know that you have asked, it is given and allow yourself to receive it. It will come on Divine schedule.

When it comes to attracting into our lives what we want, we have to realize that this is a spiritual and metaphysical law. It is happening all the time, whether we realize it or not. We do not create anything. We cannot will anything, we have to accept into our lives, not demand. A power greater than we are does the creating. This power manifests what we are prepared to accept. If you think there is not enough and you don't have enough of what there is, you will be setting up opposition in your experience rather than cooperation. If you realize and know there is abundance all around you, and accept that fact, then you are cooperating; therefore, you are ready to accept what comes to you. Ask, know, believe, and accept all with gratitude for the magnificence of Source's generous love. Then, let go and let God. Nothing is achieved through a force of will, it is achieved by confidence and acceptance of a power greater than you are. Manifestation will come according to which thought is prevalent. If we feel we are working toward success in something but are continually revisiting it or thinking about all the stumbling blocks we encounter, we may not get the success we're planning on. If our thoughts are continually on what we don't have and what we don't want or what we feel is lacking, we can't be surprised when our desires don't come to us. Give your attention to the reality of already having the essence of what you desire. Everything has already been created it is up to us to relax, with gratitude, into the knowing we will be provided with what we desire.

CHAPTER FORTY-THREE

There are no coincidences in the people we meet and the events we experience in our lives. We attract everyone and everything to us, whether we do it consciously or unconsciously. We are a network of interacting people and events in our lives that weave the web of whom we become. We have to decide the quality of the fabric that is woven. It is going to be a roughly textured fabric like burlap or a fine silk? Canvas or cashmere? Then another question comes about. Is silk better than burlap, canvas better than cashmere? The answer is no, not at all, they are different. There is a value to all four fabrics, just as there is a value to every living thing on this earth. We are all different, yet possess something that is the same – our source. How rich the tapestry of the world will be when we realize not only our value but the value of all others. When we incorporate all of the threads of humanity into one piece of fabric, how much richer all those threads will be together than they were separately. I truly believe that God did not create the diversity that exists so that we can maintain a separation, but to let us see that there is a unity interwoven in the diversity. When any one thread in a tapestry is damaged, the integrity of the entire work is compromised. So it is with the diversity on Earth. When any one species is damaged, or any individual of that species, our planet suffers. We damage ourselves when we damage others. We humans share more commonality than we do differences. Separateness is encouraged by our governments, politics, and educational systems as well as our religious and social organizations. Any organization that excludes others is encouraging separation rather than unity or oneness.

We worry so much about what others think of how we look and what we have that we are missing satisfaction in life. I think about this because I struggled with it and still do. My thoughts of how people perceived me has always been a source of many of my problems in life. I have been so concerned with how my body has looked and what I perceived as missing in my life that I was never satisfied. I feel now the purpose of life is to reach for the highest ideal of who we are. That can be gained by love, service, and gratitude. With these three ideals working in our lives, everything else falls into place. We don't need to work on a "magic formula." Love, service, and gratitude are the formula. The highest vibrations are a part of us when we love, serve, and express gratitude. Love all, serve everyone you meet in some way, and be thankful for every minute of every day for all you receive. When we do this, we will see that we get only the best that life has to offer. This is a quote often attributed to Mother Teresa that very eloquently sums up our purpose:

> People are often unreasonable and self-centered.
> Forgive them anyway.
> If you are kind, people may accuse you of ulterior motives.
> Be kind anyway.
> If you are honest, people may cheat you.
> Be honest anyway.
> If you find happiness, people may be jealous.
> Be happy anyway.
> The good you do today may be forgotten tomorrow.
> Do good anyway.
> Give the world the best you have and it may never be enough.
> Give your best anyway.
> For you see, in the end, it is between you and God.
> It was never between you and them anyway.

[The above quote was actually written by Kent M. Keith, a Harvard undergraduate for a book on student leadership. It appeared as "The Paradoxical Commandments" in 1968. Mother Teresa had it framed and hung on the wall. It was mentioned in the book: *Mother Teresa: A Simple Path,* published in 1995. As a result of this book, it has incorrectly been attributed to Mother Teresa.]

CHAPTER FORTY-FOUR

Because of the way I have lived life, relaxing has been something I have rarely done. I was usually on a mission to do this, do that, rush , rush, always going in one direction or another but not taking time to enjoy the experiences of the here and now. I have always thought the grass was greener elsewhere. There is much to be said for relaxing just where you are. It is in the relaxing that we can find peace and contentment. We can clear the cobwebs from our minds. We relax into bed to get a good night's sleep. The beach is another place where it is easy to relax, but we don't have to go any place and it doesn't have to cost money. Relaxing is another gift we are given if we allow it into our lives. After we spend time relaxing, we find our bodies, minds, and souls refreshed. Sometimes in the relaxing, we find new solutions to old problems. Coincidence? No, it is in the stillness of relaxing that Source gives us answers we have asked for. This is all meditation is, really, a relaxing of the mind and allowing for Source to give us what we are seeking.

It is a very freeing experience to find that I am creating my world. I accept only the thoughts, ideas, and perceptions that give me the world I desire. It is becoming like a self-correcting guidance system. I spend some time every morning before I get out of bed being thankful for the day ahead and whatever it holds for me. I set myself up as positively, thankfully, and expectantly as I possibly can. When something comes along to throw a chink in the day, I stop, draw the conveyor belt into my mind and start sorting my thoughts. My emotions calm and I am much more easily able to get back to a better place. My days are going much better, my moods are much better, I am enjoying life and I am finding more and more to be thankful for every day. This shift represents truth to me. It is good, it is loving, and it is no longer fear-based and depressing. If for no other reason, my feelings are telling me that my soul is experiencing more and more freedom and I am experiencing more and more joy.

The subconscious mind does what the conscious mind tells it to. The subconscious mind is really a result of all the messages that have been fed to it. We are products, unconsciously, of how we were raised, how people have reacted to us, and how we have reacted to life and all sorts of external factors. We assimilated all of this environmental side of life and incorporated it into our belief system. What we believe to be reality is based on past experiences. When an experience gave us pleasure in some way, we consciously will return to that behavior that will once again let us experience pleasure. When we experience pain, our subconscious will do the remembering of that pain and react in a way that will protect us. This is when the necessity of our conscious thoughts become so important. If we continue to react the way we have reacted to a past experience, we will continue to experience the same thing. It is when we become aware of what we're doing, when we make the effort to retrain the reactions to our subconscious that we are able to step away and above what would be and go to a better place. I am not sure we need to questions the "why" we are thinking and reacting the way we are. Anytime I have tried to questions why I am feeling the way that I am, I have seldom been able to pinpoint anything specific, anyway. We may think that it is the driver that pulls out in front of us that makes us "mad" but maybe we are already mad about a conversation we had with someone two days earlier that has been festering inside us. We need to concentrate on becoming aware that our thoughts can either leave us mired in despair and disillusionment or they can be changed and as a result our lives and experiences will change. Lao Tzu inspired us with these words," The journey of a thousand miles begins with a single step." Any journey we have in life begins with a single act. It can be something that will lead us to something we deem to be better or it can be a step toward something that will create heartache. That first step is our thought and we are able to stop and change directions at any moment in time.

I consciously choose every day what I will put into my body. My weight loss was taken step at a time, meal by meal and bite by bite, and still is. Whatever I eat now is a conscious decision. I have only those foods around that I know are good for my body, or I don't. I love bread pudding. I may get some at a restaurant. I get a small amount. If it is good, I eat it and enjoy it. If it is not good, I don't continue to mindlessly just keep eating. I stop. For a woman fighting compulsive over-eating, this is a major breakthrough. And to think it took only sixty years. If you are wanting a change in your life and you think it is not worth the effort, or it will take too long, just realize that time will pass regardless of what you choose to do. If you are wanting to go back to school, for instance, but feel that five or six years is too long to wait to get that degree, ask yourself, "If I don't go back, where will I be in five or six years?" The time will have passed and you still have not fulfilled your desire. Step by step we can complete any journey. There is no limit to what we can achieve when we believe we can and when we have faith in ourselves.

Science has proven that energy is potential matter. It is infinite in time and space. It has no beginning and no end and is everywhere at all times and all of it is anywhere at any time. If this is the case, and if oxygen, hydrogen, nitrogen, and carbon are the atoms and DNA of all living things, then everything is basically one thing and is eternally now. Science does not work with anything unknowable, so science calls this oneness infinity. Religion says that God can't be known but calls the oneness God. Infinity and God become interchangeable. God is everywhere, infinity is everywhere. Once again, we humans get so caught up in labeling everything so that someone can be right. Science and religion are not as far apart as they sometimes seem to be. It appears to me that they are two paths to the same truth.

There is one infinite intelligence. This is the only mind there is. It is pure energy and is a part of us and we are all using it. It is everywhere and it is what everything is made of. This is the universal subconscious mind. It acts on the messages it is given and works to make that message true for us. It accepts those suggestion and messages and has the ability to make truth out of any suggestion if there is belief behind it. Everything exists in that subconscious mind. It only does what it is told. It knows everything and can do anything when the ego is out of the way (an example of this is what happens during hypnosis.) It literally rearranges matter, substance, and knowledge according to what has been suggested. Nothing is impossible to this mind and it operates entirely by the messages it is fed.

This subconscious mind reasons only deductively. This means it is already aware of the spiritual and metaphysical laws and it looks for circumstances or cause. It does exactly what it is asked to do. It acts precisely and clearly in that way at all time. It works on the thoughts and messages you give it with the faith and belief of already having been accomplished.

This sounds so simple but we have to remember that our conscious mind is the one directing our subconscious mind either aware or unaware. Our conscious mind is where our ego is contained. The ego's need to be better and right relies on what it senses in the outer world. The ego has to get out of the way. Our ego will be that little voice that says, "This is silly – things don't work that way – think about the last time you were disappointed." When we let the ego think that way, then those are the thoughts that the subconscious mind attaches to. We have to send messages and thoughts clearly and brush aside any speck of doubt. We need to feel the emotions of joy and appreciation that already having the object of our desire will bring to us. God wants for us what we want. If there are consequences to those desires we will be the ones responsible, because we are getting what we have asked for.

CHAPTER FORTY-FIVE

What we have asked for may come to us in an unexpectedly different way that we have dreamed up in our minds. For example, we are dissatisfied at work and have applied for a specific job that seems perfectly suited to us. We feel we have it, know it, and are convinced of it. We don't get that job. That is when we need to be thankful and joyful, it only means that is not the job for us. We are desiring a fulfilling job with better pay. The subconscious mind of God is working for us to have our desire and that job would not have supplied us with our desire. What usually happens when we hear the news that we didn't get the job? We throw up our hands and say, "I knew it wouldn't work!" and then continue to grumble about our current job. We have interrupted the flow of energy. We have turned feelings of alignment to our source and our desire into a different direction and the subconscious mind acts on the new directive which is no longer in alignment with our desires. If you remain steadfast in the knowledge that your new job is on its way, regardless of how many jobs pass you by, with a thankful heart, it will show up. "With God, all things are possible," and that leaves nothing out. There is perfection woven into everyone's tapestry. Remember that our physical world is not our ultimate reality and we create our own experiences by our thoughts. When you can master the faith needed to see you through to the completion of achieving your desire, you will know that you are a co-creator of your life.

Everything is one thing and thought is what moves that energy into the completion of objects and circumstances in our world. The past no longer exists so we can't continue to put blame there and let our thoughts travel there. Circumstances are what they are because of our thoughts and our ego's reactions to those thoughts. We achieve our highest vibrations from blessing all those occurrences and experiences as a gift, even if we don't understand them. Future experiences will reflect our thoughts of today and what they attract to us. The only time we need to concern our thoughts with is now. The past is over and tomorrow never arrives. It is only today – now – that we have been given.

Perceptions can be deceiving. Sometimes parents called me about something their child said had happened at school. The child wasn't lying but there were aspects of their story that didn't match the observations of the adults or sometimes the other children involved. The child usually wasn't consciously omitting anything, they just perceived it differently. All of our perceptions exist in our mind and we are right in the middle of them. As we think about our perceptions as it applies in this context I think a good example is the atom and the Solar System. They are like the large and small, mirroring each other. Perhaps if we were able to look at it from an infinite perspective, the Solar System would appear atom-sized in relation to something even greater. Everything can shift as our perception of it shifts. We consciously choose how we are going to perceive any experience we have in life. If we can shift our perspective then the experience will change for us. A change in our thoughts and attitudes in any given circumstance can make that circumstance different in our experience.

Infinity has no boundaries. Source has no boundaries. In order for God to know Himself something finite was needed. The world of the relative was created and matter is currently being manifested in our lives according to the thoughts that direct our subconscious mind. As our spirit experiences, our universal subconscious expands. God is everywhere and as we read in the *Tao te Ching*, "Tao (God) is the changeless in the changing."

CHAPTER FORTY-SIX

It was Guatama Siddhartha, the spiritual teacher on whose teachings Buddhism was founded, who said, "Do not believe anything simply because you have heard it. Do not believe in anything because it is spoken and rumored by man. Do not believe anything simply because it is found written in your religious books. Do not believe in anything merely on the authority of your teachers and elders. Do not believe in traditions because they have been handed down for many generations. But, after observation and analysis when you find anything that agrees with reason and is conductive to the good and benefit of one and all, accept it and live up to it."

In December, I was getting ready to go out of town and noticed a problem with the headlights on my car. I thought I needed a bulb replaced so I took the car to the guy who changes my oil because he had replaced a tail light at one time. He checked the light, and told me it wasn't the bulb. I was about to panic but before I could, he asked me to wait a minute. He went over, picked up the phone, made a call, explained the problem then asked me if I could take it over to the auto shop and have it looked at. I said that I could, thanked him and went on my way, saying "thank you" all the way over there. I kept telling myself, "I am sure it's going to be minor and easily fixed." The guys got it in, checked it out, gave me an estimate and set up an appointment for early the following morning.

I took it to the shop the next day. They had it fixed shortly and the cost was about half of the estimate. I went out to get in the car and the lights didn't come on. I went in and told them that the lights weren't working. They checked the battery and although that wasn't the problem with the light, it did show a low battery life left. They adjusted the light, changed the battery and after I paid that bill it was still less than the original estimate. Coincidence? No, it was my desire for an enjoyable trip and that would not have included car trouble. I was given the means to have something fixed that might have resulted in a problematic trip and it was my desire to have an enjoyable trip; things worked out perfectly. I chose to look at the car trouble as a necessary step toward an enjoyable trip rather than just a problem to get upset over. This whole episode would have been viewed much differently in the past, I am 100% certain of that. I still have problems, but my attitudes about them are different. This makes the experience completely different.

Faith takes persistent work. It is the persistent drop, drop, drop of water that wears a rock away. Anytime there is an interference in faith, doubt is created and the subconscious mind takes it as a new goal. True believing that all desires can be handled without my interference is something the old, controlling Nancy had a difficult time giving up. It is when we give up the struggle, accept what is, and ease into the flow of life that things begin working for us rather than against us. In spiritual law, faith must precede everything. The rewards are more than worth the effort and it has gotten easier and easier as I strengthen that faith. When we set up patterns of thoughts whatever is akin to this pattern is attracted and unlike patterns are rejected. If I want to attract positive experiences that is what my patterns of thought have to become. Whatever we consciously think, believe, and give our attention to is what comes our way.

CHAPTER FORTY-SEVEN

Once a new year starts, it seems that we often put that generous spirit back in our pocket to be dusted off again after Thanksgiving to be used only once a year. With this on my mind, I began thinking about helping others. The very act of generously allowing others to express themselves as who they are expands our own soul and helps us to be who we really are. A case in point was a link posted by my son, Andrew, on Facebook.

Andrew is an Eagle Scout and my seven year old grandson, Elijah, is currently in cub scouts. Andrew's experiences in scouting gave him a chance to be accepted by his peers and learn a great value system of all working together to achieve common goals. Because his father was gay and I was filled with hate at that time, I felt it also gave him some excellent role models. He was in a great troop. I knew a couple of the leaders and they provided the boys with a lot of camping experiences that the leaders of other troops didn't provide. He stated in his open letter that because of this link, even thought he was an Eagle Scout, he had serious doubts about continuing his support of Boy Scouts of America. I read the link and it concerned a troop of cub scouts that had attempted to bypass the current philosophy of allowing gay troop leaders with some creative language. Boy Scouts of America had become aware of this and notified the troop that because there was a Lesbian mother helping (her seven year old son was a member of the troop) if that continued they would lose certification. I was appalled I am thankful that our son has the value system he does that makes him want to take a stand for justice and fairness. I understand prejudice and how unfair it can be. To think this woman was deemed ineligible because of her sexual orientation makes no more sense than if I had been deemed ineligible because I was fat. I had also seen on the judging side of the fence and I now knew how wrong I had been. People judge. They judge on size, skin color, even hair color (remember the old Clairol commercial – Is it true blondes have more fun?) Remembering the Tao – the journey of a thousand miles begins with a single step, I am finding it easier to take a stand for any action that serves to make everyone see their value and oneness.

The following letter was written by Andrew as the BSA were reviewing their exclusive clauses as they applied to gay membership and leadership:

"Dear Boy Scouts of America:

I am writing to you today to offer my thoughts on your upcoming Feb. 6th vote regarding lifting the national ban on homosexuals serving in Scouts. As an Eagle Scout and a father, the current discriminatory practices of the Boy Scouts of America – specifically the bans on homosexuals and Atheists – has been deeply troubling to me. This stance has affected me strongly, because my father is a homosexual. My parents divorced when I was young and my father lived in a nearby town, so for much of my formative years the primary male influences in my life were the Scouting leadership. My father, a teacher with a distinguished career of educating and mentoring young people, was not allowed to take part in this extremely influential part of my life. I couldn't ever invite him to come on the occasional trips.

I fully support the Boy Scouts of America's effort to protect youth in their care from harm, but open homosexuals are not threats in this area. Molesters and predators are not open about their sexual preferences, they use secrecy as a means of preying on victims. An open homosexual who is leading a Scout troop would have an even stronger vested interest in making sure that nothing happens to any of the youths under his charge. And the idea that Lesbian mothers are "any" threat to male youths is absolutely ludicrous on any level.

As someone with family members and close friends who are homosexuals, I have wrestled with the decision of how to proceed in relation to Scouting now that I am a father. My wife and I have discussed it frequently. Our son is in Cub Scouts, which was a very difficult choice for us. I have seriously considered returning my Eagle Scout badge in protest. We both, however strongly believe in the core values that Scouting represents. We believe that the organization is an absolute benefit to youth.

We also feel however, that one of the values which needs to be embraced more fully is inclusiveness, which I feel is implicit in virtues of Helpfulness, Friendliness, Courteousness, Kindness, and Bravery (and, for many religions at least) Reverence. We want to be involved in leadership roles within the Scouting organization, but cannot in good faith do this if we would be forced to enforce exclusionary policies to which we object.

The values that are offered by scouting are critically important to the youth of our nation. Children of Gay and Lesbian couples, as well as gay youths themselves, deserve equal access to this organization. There may be difficulties and challenges in handling the logistics of such an inclusion in a way that is equitable, but if Scouting is to continue to thrive and to maintain its position as an organization that represents American values, it must change this policy. Otherwise, it will wither away as an archaic reflection of antiquated prejudices… and rightly so.

I urge you to make the right decision for the future of the Boy Scouts of America and if you do, know that my family and I will be proud to be associated with this organization."

When we incorporate our highest feelings into actions that support those feelings, we cannot help but draw to us only the most positive experiences. My ego says to him," NO!! Don't give up the badge, it represents accomplishment." But my soul says to him, "Do what you need to do to express the highest self of who you really are." So far, my soul is winning, and, so is his.

CHAPTER FORTY-EIGHT

Forgiveness heals. I understood the importance of this when I truly apologized to my former husband. In his graciousness, he accepted and I was able to release myself from the guilt of all the venom I had spewed during the divorce and in the years since. We had achieved a truce of sorts over the years, but the heaviness of how I had treated him was still there. That heaviness hit full force when he worked to help me see Cheyenne, but I only thanked him sincerely. As I began changing my attitudes on many things, I recognized that I would never experience peace if I did not do all that I possibly could do to right the wrong I felt I had committed. I had judged, criticized, and condemned with ferocity. There was someone else who was deserving of an apology, the father of my granddaughter.

When my daughter, Allison, was growing up she never did have marriage and raising children on her mind the way some girls do. When she was in her early twenties she had some health issues that might have taken the decision to have children away from her. Once she got over the problems, she told me that she might decide to have a baby sometime, but for me not to expect her to get married. Okay, I was a modern mother, and my view of marriage was not the best so I really didn't have a problem with that. I did tell her that she needed to get back in school and get a good job before she made a decision like that because children were not cheap to raise.

Jump ahead a few years later and I got a call from Andrew. He and Amber were going to be married. He told me I could tell Allison if I talked to her before he did. Well, being female, I hung up from him and dialed Allison to tell her that Amber and Elijah would be joining the family. . She told me that there would not be two additions to the family but three before the end of the year was over, she was pregnant. She had not gone back to school and was working at an Indian restaurant and barely making ends meet, financially. I was still happy, but concerned. I found out that this was a planned pregnancy and the baby's father was named Kenny. I told her I would like to meet him if they would want to come to Vincennes. She informed me that he really wasn't in to all "that family stuff." Another "oookay," I decided I never had to meet him if that was the way he wanted it, but it set the tone for me to find fault.

While visiting Allison, she shared stories of verbal abuse from Kenny and I decided I didn't like him at all. With her hormones jumping around and my desire to control and get her away from him, it was a rough time. She had never professed to be in love with Kenny; they had just decided to have a child together. The only positive thing I could see happening (aside from a new grandchild) was that she had returned to school to get an associate degree in phlebotomy. We continued to communicate and I hoped that things would get better when the baby girl arrived. When the situation came to a head, she was close to delivery and I seriously wondered if I would even know when she went to the hospital. The morning of November 30th arrived and I got a call from Allison that they had named their little girl Cheyenne. I breathed a sigh of relief and told her I would call her later. When I called about noon to see what time that afternoon would be a good time to visit, she refused to see me. I remember thinking that I would just go down the next day. It didn't happen, nor the day after that.

Even though I was not allowed to see Cheyenne, Allison and I still talked. I would ask questions about Cheyenne. She offered no information unless I asked. I had not even seen pictures. I was still in ignorance of how my actions had been the cause of all the heartache I was going through and I still blamed Kenny. I viewed him as the face of evil. After I got to see Cheyenne, things became a bit better, but every time I saw her, I wondered when, or if, I would see her again. I thought that if Allison and Kenny had kept me from her at birth, it could happen again.

I realized that I could not keep living that way. I decided if I was truly going to be a grandmother, I would move to Anderson and be near Andrew. I had Elijah and by that time Gideon was on his way, so I made the move. By this time, Don had moved to Evansville and Allison and Cheyenne were living with him. Kenny was involved in Cheyenne's life and was good about taking care of her and working a schedule out with Allison for her school time and work time. He had a house and was providing a home for Cheyenne also. I began to look beyond what I had thought about him to what was best for Cheyenne.

After I had apologized to Don, I realized that forgiveness and apologizing were flip sides of the same coin. When we apologize for our actions to someone else, it is in the apology that we are acknowledging that we are the ones who need forgiveness. We can offer forgiveness only when someone asks for an apology. There are many instances when someone does something that you feel they need to apologize for so that you can forgive them. It may never happen. You will find peace when you forgive, regardless. Do not hold grudges, do not blow up other's actions as being against you. When people do something unkind to you, it is a reflection of who they are and usually has nothing to do with you. Apologies to others provide the only path to forgiveness of ourselves. Because my thoughts, feelings, and views had changes so drastically, I wanted Kenny to know that I was sorry that I had treated him so badly. Yes, you will say, I went through Hell, I should expect him to apologize to me. Why? I drew all of that experience to me as the result of my actions. I was the cause of the results that I received. I had not done one thing that ever gave him a chance to react to me differently. It is when we accept total responsibility for what we get in life that we can lead a joyous, peaceful, and content life. I will repeat… when we forgive others, it doesn't have anything to do with forgiving them, it has to do with apologizing for our actions and, in essence we are asking for their forgiveness. I had judged, criticized and condemned him. He has been a good father to Cheyenne and he deserved to hear it. If there were other issues, they were no longer in my area of concern.

I had Allison call Kenny and see if it would be okay if we came by at work for me to talk to him for a minute. When we pulled into the parking lot, it dawned on me that it was there I had first met him and thought it was appropriate that this was where we were meeting now. When he came out, I commented that this was where we had our first conversation, he had thought about that, too. I told him how sorry I was for judging him, criticizing him, and condemning him. I told him that I thought he was a good daddy for Cheyenne and that was my only concern and always had been. I confessed that I knew I had been mean and hateful and I had never given him a chance. I had never given him a reason to give me a chance as well. He thanked me for the apology and said he appreciated it. We talked about Cheyenne and laughed about some of the stuff she did. Before Allison and I left, I hugged him and thanked him again. I am not sure who was more surprised, Allison or Kenny. His new girlfriend was there and I told her how much I appreciated how well she treated Cheyenne. It gave all of us a chance to put to rest old wrongs and resentments.

CHAPTER FORTY-NINE

Our egos take upon themselves situations that are not even something we should be dealing with, much less trying to control. Our egos cause us to stick our noses into other people's business and try to figure out what is best for them. Every person has the right to sort those things out for themselves. If they make decisions that are not in their best interests, it is up to them to do something about it, not us. They are attracting to themselves their own experiences, as are we. Egos need to control, and that is what mine tried to do, and did. Even when I felt that things spun out of control, my ego kept me going to gain control. That does not mean that I don't have some concern for others; it means that I put those concerns in the proper place and bless them.

When we understand that what we do to others, we do to ourselves, we no longer want to treat them badly. When we understand what is appropriate, we make sure that the ego is no longer an unruly child. It is in the past and it does no good for me to spend time trying to decide what I would do differently. I did what I did and I was responsible for the consequences. The effects were those that I drew to myself by my thoughts and actions. Allison's life is not what I had hoped it would be when she was a child but it is her life. Forgiveness is that nudge we get from the God of our understanding that we are beginning to remember our unity with Him. We can't presume to be close to the essence of Oneness when we continue to insist upon being right. When I was a child, I learned to say, "I'm sorry." My apologies were for hurting someone's feelings with an unkind word, not an apology for saying the unkind words to begin with. I was apologizing for the effect, not the cause. My apologies to both Don and Kenny were an apology for both my words and my actions toward them.

Everything operates according to the laws of cause and effect. Negative actions on our part cannot cause anything but a negative effect. Likewise, when any action comes from love and kindness, the effect will be positive. If we want to change our life experiences, we have to change our thinking. We always get what we ask for, whether we realize we are asking for it or not. The mind of Source has no limitations.

Jesus had to have been a disappointment to the Jews of his time. They were all expecting someone to come charging in and set up an earthly kingdom and smite all the enemies. Jesus came with love and compassion, he treated those around him with kindness. He talked to those deemed unfit by society of the day. He outraged the religious leaders. He left no one out. Everyone was equal in his eyes as they were in God's eyes. He was the embodiment of God on earth and he tried to tell us that is what is expected of us too. When the consciousness of enough people change, the consciousness of the earth will shift and the world will be more peaceful. We are beginning to see that shift. When enough people make choices for the good of all sentient beings on the planet, corporations that are engaged in unhealthy practices will have to make a shift. The plant and animal life on the planet will breathe a collective sigh of relief. When we see negative circumstances happen, and they will, we cannot accept this as our final reality. It is only when we accept the negative as real that it becomes real. If we view those circumstances as a step on the path toward our desire then they will remain only temporary.

As I have developed a more conscious way of thinking, I realize that it is the direction of our thoughts that give meaning to any given circumstance or experience. We can accept that there will be tragedies in our lives. Our grief over losses can be accepted and resolved in a positive way. In the acceptance of this, we can realize that what is happening on the physical plane is only temporary. How we allow events to shape us define us. When there are events of nature that go beyond explanation, the only option we have is to acknowledge the event, accept it, and move on as positively as possible. It is then that working toward the highest vibrational emotion is the best course of action for you and those around you. We cannot change the events once they happen.

A change in awareness goes beyond positive thinking. The problem with positive thinking alone is that it is usually ego-based. We think that it will solve our problems. When things start to get rough, we usually abandon our positive thoughts. We usually think those thoughts for only as long as they are working for us. If we consciously pick our thoughts, monitor them, and accept only those that will resound vibrationally to the highest emotions, then we will have good drawn to us. This won't happen quickly, it will take practice, it will take focused attention, but it will happen. When you are in this place of higher emotions, you will be able to cope positively with tragedies.

CHAPTER FIFTY

When I first began this journey my concern was for material gain. Even though I was reading that there was great abundance and that our lives could be more than we had ever realized, I did not fully buy into it. I wanted my life fulfilled the way I wanted it fulfilled and I thought more money was the answer. I was still wanting to call the shots and control my future. Am I still waiting for money to come raining down on me? No, I am not. I am content with exactly what I have. I know that whatever I need will be here for me when I need it. Does that give me a ticket to be lavish and extravagant with myself? No, it gives me the ticket to be of service to others and to share what I have with someone who needs it more than I do. The more I give of myself and what I am blessed enough to receive, the more I gain in return and the better I feel about myself and the world around me. That is a gift. That is my abundance.

When we live a life of dissatisfaction, no amount of money or luxury can satisfy us. When we accept and rejoice in who we are and where we are in our lives right now, everything in life is satisfying. We're thankful for it all. It is truth and we know it. Our soul knows it. Everything our eyes fall on is a source of wonder and amazement.

The following fictional story, originally written by Elizabeth Silance Ballard but widely circulated across the internet, exemplifies the effects of kindness on many different levels:

As she stood in front of her 5th grade class on the very first day of school, she told the children an untruth. Like most teachers, she looked at her students and said that she loved them all the same. However, that was impossible, because there in the front row, slumped in his seat, was a little boy named Teddy Stoddard.

Mrs. Thompson had watched Teddy the year before and noticed that he did not play well with the other children, that his clothes were messy and that he constantly needed a bath. In addition, Teddy could be unpleasant.

It got to the point where Mrs. Thompson actually would take delight in marking his papers with a broad red pen, making bold X's and then putting a big "F" at the top of his papers.

At the school where Mrs. Thompson taught, she was required to review each child's past records and she put Teddy's off until last. However, when she reviewed his file, she was in for a surprise.

Teddy's first grade teacher wrote, "Teddy is a bright child with a ready laugh. He does his work neatly and has good manners, he is a joy to be around."

His second grade teacher wrote, "Teddy is an excellent student, well-liked by his classmates, but he is troubled because his mother has a terminal illness and life at home must be a struggle."

His third grade teacher wrote, "His mother's death has been hard on him. He tries to do his best, but his father doesn't show much interest and his home life will soon affect him if some steps aren't taken."

His fourth grade teacher wrote, "Teddy is withdrawn and doesn't show much interest in school. He doesn't have many friends and he sometimes sleeps in class."

By now, Mrs. Thompson realized the problem and she was ashamed of herself. She felt even worse when her students brought her Christmas presents wrapped in beautiful ribbons and bright paper, except for Teddy's. His present was clumsily wrapped in the heavy, brown paper that he got from a grocery bag. Mrs. Thompson took pains to open it in the middle of the other presents. Some of the children started to laugh when she found a rhinestone bracelet with some of the stones missing, and a bottle that was one-quarter full of perfume. But she stifled the children's laughter when she exclaimed how pretty the bracelet was, putting it on, and dabbing some of the perfume on her wrist. Teddy Stoddard stayed after school that day just long enough to say, "Mrs. Thompson, today you smelled just like my Mom used to" after the children left, she cried at least an hour.

On that very day, she quit teaching reading, writing, and arithmetic. Instead, she began to teach children. Mrs. Thompson paid particular attention to Teddy. As she worked with him, his mind seemed to come alive. The more she encouraged him, the faster he responded. By the end of the year, Teddy had become one of the smartest children in the class, and despite her lie that she would love all the children the same, Teddy became one of her "teacher's pets."

A year later, she found a note under her door, from Teddy, telling her that she was still the best teacher he ever had in his whole life.

Six years went by before she got another note from Teddy. He then wrote that he had finished high school, third in his class, and she was still the best teacher he ever had in his life.

Four years after that, she got another letter, saying that while things had been tough at times, he'd stayed in school, had stuck with it, and would soon graduate from college with the highest of honors. He assured Mrs. Thompson that she was still the best and favorite teacher he had ever had in his whole life.

Then four more years passed and yet another letter came. This time he explained that after he got his bachelor's degree, he had decided to go a little further. The letter explained that she was still the best and favorite teacher he ever had. But now his name was a little longer...the letter was signed, Theodore F. Stoddard, MD.

The story does not end there. You see, there was yet another letter that spring. Teddy said he had met this girl and was going to be married. He explained that his father had died a couple of years ago and he was wondering if Mrs. Thompson might agree to sit at the wedding in the place that was usually reserved for the mother of the groom.

Of course, Mrs. Thompson did. And guess what? She wore that bracelet, the one with several rhinestones missing. Moreover, she made sure she was wearing the perfume that Teddy remembered his mother wearing on their last Christmas together.

They hugged each other and Dr. Stoddard whispered in Mrs. Thompson's ear, "Thank you Mrs. Thompson for believing in me. Thank you so much for making me feel important and showing me that I could make a difference."

Mrs. Thompson, with tears in her eyes, whispered back. She said, "Teddy, you have it all wrong. You were the one who taught me that I could make a difference. I didn't know how to teach until I met you."

Anytime we allow ourselves the luxury of caring and making a difference in the life of anyone else, we will receive more back than we could ever fathom. There are ripples that radiate from acts of kindness. Those ripples reach wider and wider as those who receive kindness are kind to others. We all have the potential to make a lasting positive contribution to the lives of others if we will be kind. The next story reminds us of how important love is:

A woman came out of her house and saw three old men with long white beards sitting in her front yard. She did not recognize them. She said, "I don't think I know you but you must be hungry. Please come in and have something to eat."

"Is the man of the house home?" they asked. "No," she said, "he's out." "Then we cannot come in," they replied. In the evening when her husband came home, she told them what had happened. "Go tell them I am home and invite them in." The woman went out and invited the men in. "We do not go into a house together."

"Why is that?" she wanted to know. One of the old men explained, "His name is Wealth," he said pointing to one of his friends, and said pointing to another one, "He is Success, and I am Love." Then he added, "Now go in and discuss with your husband which one of us you want in your home."

The woman went in and told her husband what was said. Her husband was overjoyed. "How nice!!" he said. "Since that is the case, let us invite Wealth. Let him come and fill our home with wealth!" His wife disagreed. "My dear, why don't we invite Success?" Their daughter-in –law was listening from the other corner of the house. She jumped in with her own suggestions, "Would it not be better to invite love? Our home will then be filled with love!" "Let us heed our daughter-in-law's advice," said the husband to his wife. "Go out and invite Love to be our guest."

The woman went out and asked the three old men, "Which one of you is Love? Please come in and be our guest." Love got up and started walking toward the house. The other two also got up and followed him. Surprised, the lady asked Wealth and Success, "I only invited love, why are you coming? The old men replied together, "If you had invited Wealth or Success, the other two of us would've stayed out, but since you invited love, wherever he goes, we go with him. Wherever there is love, there is also wealth and success!!"

The final story is one of which we all need to be reminded time to time:

One day, a rich man told his son that he was taking him to the countryside to show him how poor a person can be. The son agreed happily. They stayed in a hut on the farm for a whole day. When they came back, the man asked his son if he liked the trip. The boy replied, "Yes, I liked it very much. We have a pool that extends to the garden but they have a whole creek which is endless. We have one dog but they have a whole lot of animals. We have a small garden but they have a whole farm. We have imported lamps but they have all the stars and the moon. Our patio reaches the front yard but they have the whole beautiful horizon. Thank you, Dad, for showing me how poor we are." After that, his father was speechless.

CHAPTER FIFTY-ONE

Perceptions of society and the ego can cause us to be puffed up with our importance. When we become observers we can see the abundance around us that has little to do with material wealth. When we finally understand what is important to the spirit, and strive for that joy, all other things will be given to us.

Jesus said, "Thou shall love the lord thy God with all thy heart and with all thy soul and with all thy mind. This is the first and greatest commandment. And the second is like unto it, "Thou shall love they neighbor as thyself." Paul wrote that if we understand everything, have all knowledge and all faith, if "I have not love I am nothing...Faith, Hope, Love... the greatest of these is love." Love overcomes fear, hate, everything. To love is our nature but fear keeps it locked inside us. You can see love in the rain as well as the flowers. When we let love work in our lives as a power for good, we express it through kindness, compassion, and a generous spirit toward others. When we lack love we become selfish, bitter and hateful. Love is all around us, all we have to do is open our heart and let it flow to us and through us.

For thirty years I felt rejected, hurt, and unloved. It was when I opened my heart that I was able to overcome my fears of life and be ready to accept all love that **is** life. Every day of our lives we are able to choose, accept, and allow love to come to us. We must love and we must allow love into our lives. There is no limit to love in the universe and it is when we allow it to flow through us that the door to everything good and positive is opened.

Just as our ego causes us to limit everything in life, so too it causes us to limit our idea of what love is. If I define love as having a man love me, I am without that; therefore, the ego says that I am without love. When I married, I loved my husband. I thought I did, therefore I did, as I knew how. I based that "love" on my need for "completion." I saw him as a way of supplying me with the things I lacked. When conditions are put on love for fulfillment, we learn to give love in exactly the same way – with conditions. When my husband expressed who he was, it did not coincide with my need, therefore the love quickly turned into something else. We have to be open to love in all forms for us to feel the full force of it.

CHAPTER FIFTY-TWO

An acquaintance called to say that his promised materials would be late; his son had died. My heart went out to him; his son was only thirty-eight, two years older than my son. There are no words to ease that grief. It is never easy to physically give up those we love. To know we will never be able to hug them again, smile at them and hear their laugh causes us to fear death. We fear for ourselves as much as we do for our loved ones. Many say that as long as they know their love one will be in Heaven, they can rest in that. Since I don't believe that hell is one of the options, that isn't my concern. It would just be about how much I miss having them around.

Never give up an opportunity to love, to show concern or to reach out to anyone who needs you. That is how love needs to work in our world. When we think of war, terrorists or criminals on death row, we think of people who are often undeserving of life. How we sell God and ourselves short when we think this way. When we can grieve with any family experiencing physical loss of a loved one, then we get closer to understanding how God loves. Condemned criminals have mothers and fathers who grieve their loss. Those terrorists we choose to hate so much were once cute babies laughing with their families. Those "enemies" loved and were loved before they realized they would one day be called upon to go to war and fight and kill others.

Many years ago I came to believe in reincarnation. When I found that Don was gay I was reading what I could find on homosexuality to try and come to some understanding. I had a friend who was into reincarnation. She gave me some books to read and in one of those, I found some interesting facts, one of which was that about 25% of all people worldwide believe to some degree in reincarnation. I read passages that discussed how the spirit may not be out of our body very long before it goes into another physical being. If that is the case, and you had a musical adult who incarnated into another body without having lost the memory of that talent, it could result in a child with a propensity toward early musical achievement or what we would dub a "child prodigy." They simply have a remembrance from a past life. They already have the knowledge from that life that they are bringing into their new life. It seemed, at the time, to explain homosexuality. If a spirit were of one gender and came back into a different gendered sentient being, they might bring that gender association with them.

It gave me the first glimpse that if reincarnation was a possibility then Hell was not a possibility. Maybe when we die our spirit has a time to reflect on all life's experiences and then can decide to comeback for another life. I have come to realize that all was created and waiting to be made manifest, therefore, reincarnation makes sense. God doesn't see us a failing. If our soul's desire is to expand then that experience might very well involve more than one incarnation. We can come back time and time again if we choose. When our time in this physical body is over our spirit continues and is freed from this finite encapsulation. Perhaps the "many rooms in the mansion" that the Bible refers to is all that bodies that our soul will be able to experience.

One hundred percent of the time when we hear something or see something we formulate an opinion about it. When those opinions are revisited in our mind again, we begin thinking more about them. When we have thoughts over and over about the same topic and continue to think of them in the same way, we come to believe them. When we believe something to be "truth" for long enough, it then becomes incorporated into our belief system. What our belief systems tell us and the way in which they shape us is where we put our faith. If that is the case, then we can say the reverse. Our faith is something we have come to believe based on our thoughts and opinions. That may sound rather simplistic and understated, but I don't think we need to make life any more complicated. Look at the way people react to each other and you can see the truth of it. We have the opinion that we are separate, this is what we allow our thoughts to let us believe. It is when we begin to shift our thoughts that our opinions change. When our thoughts change, we question our belief systems. When our belief systems change, the truth becomes revealed to us in the way we feel. It is in the feelings we have that we know truth. When we reach that place where we know something beyond a shadow of a doubt because of our feelings that we achieve our truth.

CHAPTER FIFTY-THREE

Cause and effect is a law, unshakable because it is always at work. The Law of Attraction is cause and effect working in our lives. It works at all times. Whether we accept or reject truths doesn't mean they are not happening. If we continue to allow our subconscious mind to take over and control our lives without any input from us, it is a choice we make daily. It is when we take the responsibility for our thoughts consciously that we can create miracles with our own lives. Our lives become joyous daily events. Problems that arise are more easily solved because we have the system. This system is always working; now in our favor, guiding us through life.

Our thoughts and opinions are unique to each of us, yet as they are interwoven with thoughts of others, their energy increases exponentially. As surely as like atoms are attracted to form matter, so too do we become attracted to those who share our thoughts and opinions. That is how we establish relationships of all kinds. As our thoughts change we will notice that our circle of friends and acquaintances reflect that change. It is when we cast out our fear of life and embrace all the world has to offer that we begin to live a fulfilled life.

When I was trying to think of a really good example to illustrate how our conscious and subconscious work, the closest analogy I could come up with was a compute game. When you have a disc, for a chess game, you put it in the computer and download it to the hard drive. You can then remove the disc and play the game of chess. It doesn't matter what move you make, the computer will go to its memory of all possible moves and pick the one to counter yours and the game goes on. Every move the computer makes is based on your move and the input from the hard drive. All the possibilities are in the hard drive, waiting for your move to command it. This is how the conscious and subconscious work to present you with your reality. As your thoughts are realized the subconscious goes to work to counter the thought you have given to it. Whatever we feed into our subconscious mind with our thoughts is what it will act upon. All the subconscious does is create and it creates from our thoughts. My subconscious has been creating for me without my knowledge and direction for over sixty years. Now that I know how it works, I am able to direct it to create what I desire. By attuning my feelings vibrationally, I am ready to accept what I will be given.

Every moment of every day we are living an expression that reflects who we are. We are not only our bodies. Who we really are is a spiritual, divine part of Source and we share that with everything on the planet. Our thoughts, words and actions define us to the external world. We have the potential to create ourselves anew every moment of every day. We can do this unconsciously, as I did my entire life, or consciously, as I have become aware and am deciding now. Previously, I thought that I was who I was based on my parents' messages, commercial television messages and other peoples' reactions to me…. All outer expressions by other people. Now, I know that I am the one creating this person called Nancy. When we make a deliberate choice of our thoughts and speak in a way that encourages harmony, then act in a way that is beneficial to ourselves and others, we are beginning to express the highest version of ourselves. No matter what, we do not become anything other than an eternal spirit. That is what we are and always will be. It is when we express the best and highest version of ourselves that we will experience the peace, joy and love that our soul longs for.

The following is a text from *The Temple of Understanding*.

The Golden Rule

Aboriginal Spirituality – "We are as much alike as we keep the Earth alive." – Chief Dan George

Islam – "Not one of you truly believes until you wish for others you wish for yourself." = The Prophet Muhammed, Hadith

Baha'I Faith – "Lay not on any soul a load that you would not wish to be laid upon you and desire not for anyone the things you would not desire for yourself." – Gaha'u'llah, Gleanings

Jainism – "One should treat all creatures in the world as one would like to be treated." – Mahavira. Suttakritanga

Buddhism – "Treat not others in ways that you yourself would find hurtful." – The Buddha, Udana-Varga 5.18

Judaism – "What is hateful to you, do not do to your neighbor. This is the whole Torah, all the rest is commentary." – Hillel, Talmud, Sabbath 31a

Christianity – "In everything, do to others as you would have them do to you, for this is the law of the prophets." – Jesus, Matthew 7:12

Sikhism – "I am a stranger to no one and no one is a stranger to me. Indeed, I am a friend to all." – Guru Granth Sahib, pg. 1299

Confucianism – "One word which sums up the basis of all good conduct…loving kindness. Do not do to others what you do not want done to yourself." Confucius, Anatects 15:23

Taoism – "Regard your neighbor's gain as your own gain and your neighbor's loss as your own loss." – Tai Shang Kan Ying P'ien 213-218

Zoroastrianism – "Do not do unto others whatever is injurious to yourself." – Shayast-na-Shayast 13-29

We are all of one mind regardless of culture, religion or nationality. When we see the similarities and get beyond the need to collect and convert others to our own way of thinking, there is much unity. Teachers have been sent throughout the ages and to all corners of the planet to help us understand this concept.

CHAPTER FIFTY-FOUR

One day I went to church with Andrew and Amber and heard the minister ask us to think about this: You receive $525,600. You will be given this amount yearly. You will get the interest on it only, you must give it all away. How will you give it? I was sitting there thinking about how much fun it would be to have that much money to give away every year to causes and people who could use the kind of help that much money could provide. He then said, "The reason for that specific amount is that it is the number of minutes in a year. How will you spend it, knowing you get to keep the interest on it only?" When I think of how I spend the minutes of my life, am I giving them in a way that will create a lasting "deposit of interest?"

An old Cherokee is teaching his grandson about life, "A fight is going on inside me," he said to the boy.

It is a terrible fight and it is between two wolves. One is evil – he is anger, envy sorrow, regret, greed, arrogance, self-pity, resentment, inferiority, lies, false pride, superiority, and ego." He continued, "The other is good – he is joy, peace, love, hope, serenity, humility, kindness, benevolence, empathy, generosity, truth, compassion, and faith. The same fight is going on inside your – and inside every other person, too."

The grandson thought about it for a minute and then asked his grandfather, "Which wolf will win?"

The old Cherokee simply replied, "The one you feed."

I believe this story speaks to the universal human condition. Our inherent nature is good. Toddlers do not possess those qualities of the evil wolf. We are the good wolf from the moment we are born. As we grow older, it is the society, the culture and the environment we are in that gives rise to the evil wolf. This happens when we make errors in our thinking. When our thoughts become ego-based, it gives rise to those qualities that are deemed bad. Just as "right" and "wrong" are polar opposites, so too are "good" and "evil." They represent error. Once both wolves exist within us it is never too late to feed the good wolf. The good wolf is patient, she is always there waiting. Anytime we smile at a stranger, she is fed. As we think about and acknowledge her presence, we will become more aware of her needs. As we feed her and see that her love improves the quality of our life, we want to give her more attention because we come to love her. For, you see, she represents our soul, the part of Source that is within. As we feed her and love her, she grows stronger. The evil wolf moves into the background, knowing that he is no longer calling the shots.

I know there are a great many people reading this book who have had similar experiences. They have dealt with them in their own way. Wherever you are in your life's journey is the right place for you to be.

CHAPTER FIFTY-FIVE

I try to show kindness, generosity and love in dealing with others. If they perceive it differently, I cannot control that. We cannot control others. I spent a lifetime trying. It doesn't work. We control our thoughts and which ones we give attention to; and, we control our own experiences to the extent that we allow our lives to flow. When we approach our interactions with others in a negative way, it doesn't serve either party well. We give others what we see in ourselves. When we adjust our own thoughts and feelings we are able to give others the respect they deserve. We no longer want to be critical, judgmental or ill-willed. We want peace and harmony for everyone. We want others to experience a joyous life also. We come to realize that we truly desire to put the Golden Rule into effect in our lives.

At times, because of previous actions on our part or theirs, a relationship may have gone beyond something salvageable. If this is the case, when you make the attempt, you feel better and will be able to take the responsibility for your part in the break down. You will also be able to objectively reflect on the blessings that relationship afforded you while it was active. You can be grateful for the blessings of it even though it no longer exists. If you can appreciate and be thankful for the flow of people in and out of your life and appreciate and treat them kindly while they are there, you will find that your relationship longevity improves. Recognize that you have a relationship of sorts with everyone you meet. It may only be a nod and a smile, but your lives have touched for a brief instant. You are an angel. You are a gift and so are they. Enjoy the experience and be thankful for it.

One of the wonderful benefits of this way of living is the sense of empowerment you feel. One person truly can make a difference in the life of others. We all share the same desires for acceptance and camaraderie. That is what you are giving everyone when your thoughts, actions and reactions become positive. You are lifting them up and as a result are uplifted yourself. You step away from your ego and see the value of everyone. I am reminded of that little song I learned as a kid, "This little light of mine, I'm gonna let it shine." We can be a light to everyone we meet. We don't know what darkness and heartache and struggles they are having. When we are kind, that is our light.

When we are one with everyone, the need to be right disappears. We are busy being kind, happy and generous in spirit. Our life encompasses everyone where they are. We see injustices imposed upon others and want to help them in some way. We no longer wish to engage in strife with anyone over anything. We will accept that their beliefs are different from ours and just as valid. We will no longer feel the need to guide and direct them to our way of thinking.

We are all worthy of the best that life has to offer. When we are at those low emotions on the vibrational scale, we see our reality as firm and never-changing. We think that we are doomed to always being discontented, disappointed and unhappy. We get irritated easily. We look at others and think their life is problem free. We all have our struggles. All we have to do to get the life we want is to change our thoughts, feelings and reactions. When we view everything that happens to us as exactly what is supposed to happen, and view it with gratitude, we will be looking at the very things that will change. What was previously viewed as unacceptable will be but a step toward our desire. Our vibrations will stay in a higher frequency and we will be allowing those very things that we desire to continue to us.

If you want to have a more fulfilling life, consider first what you are listening to on television and the radio. Ninety percent of our media is currently owned by six corporations. Whether you are conservative or liberal, hip-hop or Lawrence Welk, or anywhere in between that range, this kind of monopoly does not encourage unbiased coverage of anything. When we pander to a bias in any way by listening to it and accepting it as fact, we can fuel our frustrations. Anything that adds disruption, confusion and promotes a "them" and "us" opposition will not serve you well if your intent is to become a higher vibrational being. It is when we become conscious of our similarities rather than our differences that we open the door to the higher emotions and vibrations. The media currently does not often promote a calmness in us. That is not to say that you need to stop watching any program whatsoever that you choose to, it is just a reminder to be more aware of how those programs you currently watch are making you feel, and what kind of thoughts they trigger. If they contribute to your feelings of contentment, harmony and happiness without leading to frustration, despair, and ill-will then they are not hindering your efforts in any way to reaching higher vibration.

CHAPTER FIFTY-SIX

To achieve a greater degree of happiness and fulfilment in your life, use these nine steps as a guideline:

STEP ONE: Begin to think about what you are thinking about. Become an observer of what thoughts roll through your mind. Decide which thoughts send you to the negative emotions and the feelings they bring out in you. Consider the positive thoughts and the feelings they encourage in you. Just start slowing them down and observing them.

The more you observe your thoughts, the easier this will become. After you have observed for a while, begin sorting those thoughts. Try to find a visual that will help you sort them. I use a conveyor belt. You might use a trash can, a big box ready to ship off to parts unknown, a sewer-pipe whatever you can come up with as a place to dump the negative thoughts. These thoughts would be **any** negative thoughts about yourself, your body, your job, your friends and family, any drama you are in the middle of, any negative circumstances whatsoever. Sort them and get rid of the ones that don't serve those higher emotions. Don't curse them thereby giving attention to them. Observe them and put them in the trash. Thank them for showing up and making themselves known to you , but kindly advise them you won't be needing them anymore and simply **let them go.**

When you have any positive thoughts, regardless of how small or large, pick those up, give them your attention, thank them for showing up and put them close to you so that you can revisit them. Revisit them often. Give them your attention and let them lift you up. I recently saw a piece of wisdom from the Facebook site "Never Give up on Yourself" and I have changed it a bit. "Look in the mirror every night and say this: "~~You are~~ I am beautiful (or handsome). ~~You are~~ I am strong. ~~You are~~ I am smart. ~~You are~~ I am loved. The next morning, you will look in the mirror and see a different person, someone who is loved, because to be loved, you must love yourself. You are all beautiful. You are all strong. You are all smart. You are all loved." The more you feed the positive thoughts and messages and starve the negative thoughts and messages, the better you will begin feeling from within.

STEP TWO: Begin reading. If you are on Facebook, look for sites that speak to you. Read books. If you don't enjoy reading, get audio books. I have included a bibliography of my reading at the end. Read biographies of people you admire or people who have worked to make the world better. Whatever inspires you personally, delve into it.

STEP THREE: Begin appreciating everything you do have, everything around you, be thankful for where you are right now. Be appreciative of nature. Take time to enjoy nature in any way you can. Listen to your favorite music. Appreciate the talent that went into providing it to the world. Sing, dance, and allow music to saturate you. Be thankful for life period. There is beauty everywhere, even in what we call imperfections, because truth knows that there are no imperfections. We are spiritual beings in a physical body, not the other way around. The physical body may be what the ego calls "imperfect" but realize that you are a perfect spirit. Our outer actions may not always reflect that, but when that happens we have what the Dalai Lama calls an "unruly ego." This too will improve. As you are grateful and appreciative for all circumstances, you will find them changing. Go to nature for inspiration. Be thankful for both the sunny days and the rainy days. Express gratitude for everything. Be thankful for all you have and everyone in your life.

STEP FOUR: Never underestimate the power of a small kindness. There is no act of kindness, regardless of how big or small that does not matter. Give your smiles away freely, even when you're not certain you have something to smile about. Hold the door open for someone or pick up a piece of litter. Say "excuse me" when you cross in front of someone's path. Tell the cashier to have a nice day. Crumble that uneaten biscuit and throw it out for the birds.

STEP FIVE: Don't be afraid – step out of fear and into love. We desire affection, love, appreciation and acceptance, regardless of who we think we are. When we give to others those things we want most will come back to us. Fear keeps us from giving of ourselves to others. We have a fear of rejection, a fear of being misunderstood, a fear that what we have is not good enough because we are not good enough. That is what ego does to us. When you step away from fear and the ego and into love, your light shines brightly to others. We are no better or worse than anyone we meet. We share the same spirit, the same universal subconscious mind and we are all only in a temporary physical body. We are a part of infinity and we are all eternal. There is empowerment in this and there is no room for fear.

STEP SIX: Start to notice how often you attach labels to people. When we do this, we are making judgments. Begin to notice how differently you treat people because of those labels you give them. When we remove labels we put everyone on the even playing field of humanity. We will treat a janitor with as much respect as we would a world leader. We see the value of each and every individual. In viewing people in this way, we realize that they are just as valuable as we are and that our value is equal to theirs. We are all valuable in the mind of God. No one person, no one race, no one religion, no one gender is any different in value.

As you notice how you label others, begin removing those labels. Remove any stereotyping of people you meet. Do not judge them by the clothes they wear or by their looks. Remove your bias. Look at them – each and every one – as though they are an angel that God sent to you as a gift. That is what they are. Then realize that you, too are an angel being sent as a gift to them. Be a kind, compassionate and uplifting gift. Be a gift of light that brightens them.

STEP SEVEN: Continue to sort your thoughts. Continue to read. Continue to be thankful for everyone and everything. Continue to be kind and generous of spirit to everyone you encounter. Continue to follow love rather than fear. Stop judging others.

STEP EIGHT: Embrace those who bring out the best in you. Don't turn away from your church or your religious beliefs; that is not what this is about. Use it as the foundation, just don't let it limit your belief of the God-power that is within each of you. Don't limit God. Let your soul expand and be free enough to accept that God is within. Begin to notice the abundance in life and be in that flow of all good things.

STEP NINE: Be patient. Be open to all possibilities. Regardless of what your senses (ego) may be trying to say, listen only to the thoughts and feelings that allow your desire to come to you. Become familiar with the power of your thoughts. Realize that opportunities to fulfill your desires will come to you in ways you can't foresee. What you first desire, pales in comparison to what you really get coming into your life. It is a fulfillment of such a great magnitude that "things" no longer hold the significance they did before.

EPILOGUE

I still look forward to every day and what it will bring. I know, more than ever, that each day is a gift. Everyone is an angel with a gift for us and we are angels with a gift for everyone we meet. There are no such things as coincidences.

I have a list of inspirational Facebook sites and a Bibliography that follow. I hope you will take advantage of both of these list. Embark on your path with an open mind and know that it will be exciting and joyous. Nothing concerns you or worries you because you come to realize that worry is using the imagination to attract what you don't want.

Live kindly, live generously and live compassionately. Smile every time you can, it is a gift that will help spirits soar. (Yours and everyone's you encounter.) Remember The Golden Rule every day in every way.

Love, love, love. Love even when it may not be returned because it is in the act of loving that we send out ripples to others. Be genuinely yourself. Don't concern yourselves with how others view you. Don't judge, don't criticize, don't condemn – and start with yourself on this one, too.

Be the best version of your highest self every moment of every day. It is when we are better today than we were yesterday that we are living up to our purpose.

Enjoy life and know that I love you all.

Nancy

INSPIRATIONAL FACEBOOK SITES

Zen to Zany
Loving Them Quotes
Relax, Relate, Release
Akashic Records
Earth. We are one
The Best Status
Smile BIG, Love Everybody
Embracing Your Best Self
Oneness Happens Here
Expanded Consciousness
From Hell to Well
Happiness Convert
Spirit, Science and Metaphysics
The road to ME
Zen-Sational Living
Paying it Forward
Living the Law of Attraction
Maya Angelou

Quantum Awakening
Waves of Gratitude
Live a Flourishing Life
Shift Happens
Neil deGrasse Tyson
Dr. Wayne W. Dyer
Success 365
Heaven and Hell
Phil Good
Cloud Nine Girl
Happy by Choice
Walking My Talk
A Course in Miracles
Nelson Mandela
40 Days of Giving
Daily Dose
Steve Maraboli
The Idealist

BIBLIOGRAPHY

1. Albom, Mitch. *Have a Little Faith.* New York City. Hyperion. 2009.
2. Anderson, Ken. *Where to Find it in the Bible.* Nashville, Thomas Nelson, Inc. 1996.
3. Anderson, Uell S. *Three Magic Words.* USA
4. Aslan, Reza. *No god but God.* New York City. Ember, a division of Random House. 2011.
5. Batcvhelor, Stephen. *Confessions of a Buddhist Atheist.* New York City. Spiegel and Graw Trade Paperbacks. 2011.
6. Braden, Gregg. *The God Code.* New York City. Hay House. 2004.
7. Breathnach, Sarah Ban. *Simple Abundance, A Daybook of Comfort and Joy.* New York City. Warner Books. 1995'
8. Chopra, Deepak. *Creating Affluence.* San Rafael. Amber-Allen Publishing. 1998.
9. Chopra, Deepak. *The Seven Spiritual Laws of Success.* San Rafael. Amber-Allen Publishing. 1994.
10. Dyer, Dr. Wayne W. *Change Your Thoughts – Change Your Life.* New York City, Hay House, 2007.
11. Dyer, Dr. Wayne W. *Excuses Begone!* New York City, Hay House. 2009.
12. Dyer, Dr. Wayne W. *Getting in the Gap.* Carlesbad, CA. Hay House. 2009.

13. Dyer, Dr. Wayne W. *The Power of Intention.* New York City. Hay House. 2010.

14. Dyer, Dr. Wayne W. *The Shift.* New York City. Hay House. 2010.

15. Dyer, Dr. Wayne W. *Wishes Fulfilled.* New York City. Hay House. 2012.

16. Germain, Saint Series. *The I AM Discourses, Vol. 3.* Schaumburg, IL. Saint Germain Press. 2011.

17. Goddard, Neville. *The Power of Awareness.* Kindle Version.

18. Goddard, Neville. *Feeling is the Secret.* U.S. Pacific Publishing Studio. 2010.

19. Gulley, Philip and Mulholland, James. *If Grace is True.* New York City. Harper Collins. 2003.

20. Gulley, Philip and Mulholland, James. *If God is Love.* New York City. Harper Collins. 2004.

21. Gulley, Philip. *If the Church were Christian.* New York City. Harper Collins. 2010.

22. Gulley, Philip. *The Evolution of Faith.* New York City. Harper Collins. 2011.

23. Gyatso, Geshe Kelsang. *Modern Buddhism.* USA. Tharpa Publications. 2011.

24. Hawkeye, Timber. *Buddhist Boot Camp.* New York City. Harper Collins. 2013.

25. Hicks, Esther and Jerry. *Ask and It is Given.* New York City. Hay House. 2004.

26. Hicks, Esther and Jerry. *The Amazing Power of Delibrate Intent – Living the Art of Allowing.* New York City. Hay House. 2006.

27. Lama, Dalai. *Becoming Enlightened.* New York City. Atria Paperback, a division of Simon and Schuster. 2009.

28. Lama, Dalai. *Beyond Religion – Ethics for a Whole World.* Boston. Houghton Mifflin, Harcourt. 2011.

29. Lipton, Bruce. *The Biology of Belief.* New York City. Hay House. 2008.

30. Macomber, Debbie. *One Simple Act.* New York City. Simon and Schuster. 2009.

31. Macomber, Debbie. *God's Guest List.* New York City. Simon and Schuster. 2010.

32. Miller, William R. and Baca, Janet C'DE, *Quantum Change*. New York City. Guelford Press, 2001.

33. _ Ortberg, John, *The Me I Want to Be*. Grand Rapids, MI. Zondervon. 2010.

34. Schueman, Helen and Thetford, William. *A Course in Miracles*. Mill Valley, CA. Foundation for Inner Peace. 2007.

35. Tolle, Eckhart. *The Power of Now*. Canada. Namaste Publishing. 1999.

36. Tolle, Eckhart. *A New Earth*. New York City. Namaste Publishing. 2005.

37. Tolle, Eckhart. *Stillness Speaks*. New York City. New World Library. 2006.

38. Twyman, James F. *The Moses Code*. Carlsbad, CA. Hay House. 2008.

39. Walsch, Neale Donald. *Conversations with God – Book 1*. New York City. G.P. Putnam's Sons. 1995.

40. Walsch, Neal Donald. *Friendship with God*. New York City. Berkley Publishing Group. 1999.

41. Walsch, Neal Donald. *Communion with God*. New York City. Berkley Publishing Group. 2000.

42. Walsch, Neal Donald. *Happier than God*. Carlsbad, CA. Hay House. 2008.

43. Walsch, Neal Donald. *Conversations with God – Book 3*. Charlottesville. Hampton Roads Publishing Co., Inc. 2012.

44. Walsch, Neale Donald. *Conversations with God – Book 2*. Charlottesville. Hampton Roads Publishing Co., Inc. 2012.

ABOUT THE AUTHOR

Nancy Zimmerman is a lifelong teacher. After retiring from years in elementary and middle school education, she embarked on a journey of self-discovery and self-improvement; a journey that has brought her to writing this book, capturing the personal transformation in her own words.

Nancy looks forward to learning about your personal journey, as well. She can be contacted at:

nzimmie@gmail.com

https://www.facebook.com/EmbracingYourBestSelf

.

www.ingramcontent.com/pod-product-compliance
Lightning Source LLC
LaVergne TN
LVHW051514080426
835509LV00017B/2062